An Introduction to Industrial Service Design

Service design has established itself as a practice that enables industries to design and deliver their services with a human-centred approach. It creates a contextual and cultural understanding that offers opportunities for new service solutions, improving the user experience and customer satisfaction.

With contributions from leading names in the field of service design from both academia and international, professional practice, *An Introduction to Industrial Service Design* is engaging yet practical and accessible.

Case studies from leading companies such as ABB, Autodesk, Kone and Volkswagen enable readers to connect academic research with practical company applications, helping them to understand the basic processes and essential concepts. This book illustrates the role of the service designer in an industrial company, and highlights not only the value of customer experience, but also the value of employee experience in creating competitive services and value propositions. This human-centred approach brings about new innovations.

This book will be of benefit to engineers, designers, businesses and communication experts working in industry, as well as to students who are interested in service development.

Satu Miettinen is a Professor at the University of Lapland, Finland. She has been a Visiting Professor at the Centre for Design Research, Stanford University, USA, School for Design and Innovation, Tongji University, China, and the Centre for Aesthetics in Practice, Trento University, Italy. Satu has been working in service design research for several years and has authored a number of books, including *Designing Services with Innovative Methods*.

An Introduction to
Industrial Service Design

Edited by Satu Miettinen

Routledge
Taylor & Francis Group

LONDON AND NEW YORK

First published 2017 by Routledge

2 Park Square, Milton Park, Abingdon, Oxfordshire OX14 4RN
52 Vanderbilt Avenue, New York, NY 10017

Routledge is an imprint of the Taylor & Francis Group, an informa business

First issued in paperback 2019

British Library Cataloguing in Publication Data
A catalogue record for this book is available from the British Library

Library of Congress Cataloging in Publication Data
A catalog record for this book has been requested

ISBN: 978-1-4724-8577-9 (hbk)
ISBN: 978-0-367-88216-7 (pbk)

Typeset in Bembo
by Saxon Graphics Ltd, Derby

Contents

Figures

Contributors

Pelin Arslan is a leader and innovator in the global digital industry, specialising in designing services, user studies and experiences that continue to allow her to envision innovative future applications, products and services. Pelin joined Autodesk as a Service Design Manager, contributing her vision for tools, research methods and user-centred experiences. She holds a Ph.D. in Design, focusing on service design methodologies for health-care promotion, which allowed her works to be presented at international conferences and workshops. She has a double M.Sc. degree in Product Service System Design, and is one of the first graduates of the service design programme at Politecnico di Milano, and in Eco-compatible Product Design at Politecnico di Torino. She received her undergraduate degree in Industrial Design at Middle East Technical University, in Turkey. Pelin worked at the MIT Mobile Experience Lab as a research scholar and postdoctoral associate. As a project leader and service designer, she managed, coordinated and cooperated with various multidisciplinary research and business projects concerning social-media platforms, location-based services and photo/video-sharing mobile applications. Her experience also extends to researching and designing for health care and wellness, education, urban mobility and sustainability. She has worked with public institutions (the European Commission, Museum of Science, Cariplo Foundation, Tufts), as well as with large corporations (Samsung, Avea Labs, Alcatel-Lucent Bell Labs, Pirelli, Legrand, 3M, Telecom Italia).

Paula Bello's professional experience includes three key fields combining the disciplines of design thinking and business strategy: academic, corporate and entrepreneurial. She holds a Doctorate of Arts in Global Design Processes from the University of Art and Design Helsinki (now Aalto University). She has investigated how globalisation has affected design practices, and the role that design plays as a driver and mediator in a globalised world. She continues to write and publish articles. Paula Bello is also a business partner and design consultant for Livework, and has an interest in coaching enterprises to utilise design as a catalyst for change. Based on her experience, her strengths are in building strategies and facilitating dialogue to align design, technology and business. In particular, she aims to simplify the big picture and act as a bridge between people and functions, and between ideas and reality. After her doctoral research, Paula had the chance to put her theories into practice, working for more than seven years at Kone Corporation, where she led international teams tasked with building global offerings for products and services. Her last task at Kone included building the company's service design capability as the first service design manager. Currently, she is an entrepreneur in the fields of hospitality and property, directing the renewal of a century-old group of family businesses. This has led her to explore new areas of opportunity in start-ups, for which she acts as an adviser and micro-investor.

Marcus Gabrielsson and **Malin Orebäck** collaborate closely on service design projects at Veryday, one of the world's top-ranking design and innovation consultancies. Headquartered in Stockholm, with offices in New York, Shanghai, London and Dubai, Veryday holds 300 patents and has earned 220 design awards, including Red Dot Design Team of the Year. As Vice President of Business Innovation and a front-end innovation specialist, Marcus is driven by doing good; creating value and fuelling change through participatory innovation. His work on global assignments includes generating new opportunities that connect deep consumer insights with long- and short-term business objectives. A designer who has been based in Sweden, Hong Kong and New York, he has also focused on B2C and B2B incremental innovation work in the service industry. Marcus is a partner at Veryday and a member of the company's board of directors. He holds a Master of Fine Arts (MFA) degree in design.

As Vice President of Design, Malin leads the creative team with a focus on service business and customer experience. Throughout each engagement, she builds and supports multidisciplinary teams, leveraging a people-driven innovation approach to explore and uncover solutions that can make a meaningful difference to individuals, the environment, societies and businesses. A strategist with more than twenty years of consultancy experience across a wide range of industries, she is a lecturer, keynote speaker and adviser to multinational clients and global brands on customer experience, design strategy and people-driven innovation. Malin is a partner at Veryday, and holds an MFA in industrial design and an MBA in design management.

Bo Gao is Associate Professor of Service Design, Information Design, Communication Design and Sustainable Design at the College of Design & Innovation, Tongji University. In 2013, she worked as a visiting scholar at RIT, College of Imaging Arts & Sciences, USA. She is also an active member of DESIS China (Design for Social Innovation and Sustainability) and LeNS China (the Learning Network on Sustainability). She has published multiple academic papers at Cumulus (the International Association of Universities and Colleges of Art Design and Media) and Design Research Society (DRS) conferences, and delivered speeches at Lift China 2014 and 2015; Asia Consortium 2015; and the Korea Conference on Service Design 2015.

Dr Gao hosts research projects sponsored by the Social Science and Humanity Department of the Ministry of Education, China. The design work won the SEGD (Society for Experiential Graphic Design) 2014 award.

Bernadette Geuy is a design strategist and user experience lead at the University of California, Berkeley, working at the intersection of design, business and technology. Currently, she is leading the service design activities for a large-scale student systems replacement project, with a focus on transforming student journeys across a complex set of academic, administrative and financial services. She is passionate about designing services that have a strong basis in student success factors, and which facilitate good decision-making. Bernadette is a co-chair of the San Francisco chapter of the Service Design Network, which focuses on strengthening the knowledge and practice of service innovation, and her favourite activity for this group is running San Francisco's annual Service Jam. Sketching is Bernadette's superpower, and she uses it on a daily basis to problem-solve, facilitate communication, storyboard and for fun. Prior to joining UC Berkeley, she worked for many years in information technology and consulting, in a variety of roles, including engineering management, marketing and business development. Bernadette has an MBA and a BA in communications, both from UC Berkeley.

Jaana Jeminen is a project manager and expert in design management.

Titta Jylkäs is a junior researcher in service design.

Julia Kleeberger works as a design strategist with a focus on human-centred design and business innovation for Volkswagen AG. In her work, she connects user insights with foresight research, industrial product development and business insights gained through direct fieldwork, as well as through her long-lasting experience in the automotive industry, to develop innovative and interactive mobility services and products. Julia is a passionate tinkerer and believes in the wisdom of the hands, also called 'constructionism'. She is inspired daily by her own children, so it is a personal objective for her to offer kids playful access to technology – and in so doing, to develop the required skill set to solve the problems of tomorrow. Thus, she founded *Junge Tüftler,* where she runs Kinder-Hackathons and regular tinkering classes.

Yichen Lu is a doctoral candidate at the Department of Design, Aalto University. Her research topic is 'Experience Design in Business-to-Business Heavy Industry'.

Maurício Manhães works as a professor of Service Design at Savannah College of Art and Design in Savannah, Georgia, USA. He has strong interests in the management of innovative efforts, especially in the governance of innovation teams, focusing on the intersection between the service design and knowledge management fields. In 2015, he obtained a doctorate in Knowledge Management with a thesis entitled, 'Innovation and Prejudice: Designing a Landscape of Diversity for Knowledge Creation'.

He conducts workshops, lectures, classes and conferences on service innovation in several countries.

Adolfo Martini is Italian, and a graduate of contemporary history with honours from the University of Turin, Italy. He has spent more than twenty-seven years in marketing and Human Resources at L'Oreal, working in Italy, France and across Europe. Adolfo is the founder of Agility Europe Design Thinking for Business Innovation.

Tuuli Mattelmäki is an associate professor at the Department of Design in Aalto University and leader of the Encore research team that focuses on empathic design, co-design and user experience, as well as on topics related to service design.

Marjukka Mäkelä holds an MA in Industrial and Strategic Design from the University of Art and Design Helsinki (currently Aalto University). She works as a manager of industrial design and user experience. She has also studied Business Management and Marketing. Marjukka Mäkelä has worked for almost fifteen years in the machine industry, first at the elevator company Kone and currently at ABB, where she develops and coordinates design activities within the business unit of Drives and Controls. She has served as a board member of Ornamo (Finnish Association of Designers), as well as a vice president of TKO, the Finnish Association of Industrial Designers.

Satu Miettinen works as a professor of applied art and design at the University of Lapland. She has been working with service design research for several years, and has authored a number of books and research publications in this area. Her research interests are service design, including social and public service development, citizen engagement and digital service development. She works as a research lead and director for several national and international service design research projects. She has been a visiting professor at the Centre for Design Research, Stanford University in the USA, the School for Design and Innovation at Tongji University in China, and the Centre for Aesthetics in Practice, Trento University, Italy.

Susanna Nissar holds a BA in Film and an MS in Math & Computer Science from Stockholm University and the Royal Institute of Technology in Stockholm, Sweden. Susanna has always wanted to understand a variety of perspectives, as evidenced by her educational choices. She worked with user experience in digital services for several years before service design caught her eye, which was the missing piece that she had been looking for in her previous work. Until recently, Susanna was Vice President of one of Sweden's largest service design agencies, and worked with a range of clients within the private and public sectors to achieve their service design, business design and organisational design needs.

Katri Ojasalo, Ph.D., is Director of Master-level Education at Laurea University of Applied Sciences in Espoo, Finland. She completed her Ph.D.

in service productivity at the Hanken School of Economics in Helsinki, Finland, in 1999. Service businesses have been her research and development field for over twenty years, and she has published a number of journal articles, as well as several textbooks and book chapters in this field. Her current research focuses on service innovation and design, service productivity and service-based business models.

Arne van Oosterom is owner and strategic design director at DesignThinkers, a strategic design agency based in Amsterdam that specialises in new marketing and branding, social innovation, service design and customer-centred design. Arne has created a long and successful career within service design consulting and management with major corporations. On the side, he gives lectures and keynote presentations in global design at research conferences.

Katrine Rau is a senior user experience researcher for GE Energy. Her current work affects some of the world's largest energy companies. Before joining GE, she worked as a consultant, facilitating teams in various industries, including health care, retail and telecommunications, helping them to identify business challenges and solve user problems through service innovation.

Marianna Recchia is a business and service designer who loves people, food and jazz. She works at Volkswagen AG. Her previous experience is in academia and in product and service design consultancy for large companies, as well as SMEs. In addition, she was involved in social design projects aimed at testing methods of coproducing public services or investigating financing models for social housing. She is a Domus Academy alumna.

Simo Rontti (MA) is a service design project manager and lecturer at the University of Lapland, Finland. Since 2009, Rontti has been researching and developing technology-aided prototyping methods in close collaboration with dozens of case companies, such as Kone, Volkswagen and Danske Bank. Prior to that, Rontti worked for seven years as an in-house industrial designer for the Lappset Group, which operates globally in the playground equipment industry. Rontti is also a service design entrepreneur and has helped many businesses, such as those in the automotive, education and energy sectors.

Virpi Roto is a research fellow at Aalto University and a member of the Encore research team, specialising in experience-driven design in different contexts.

Reima Rönnholm is a service designer from Finland, now based and working in Singapore. He is one of the founders of Palmu, a consultancy focusing on behavioural insights, customer experience design, innovation in service production and customer-centric strategies. His past ten years working in service design have taken him around the world, from amusement parks and cruise liners to churches and African hospitals, to help those organisations learn to innovate with their customers and staff and achieve more human-centric development.

Michal Steckiw is a consultant based in London with experience in developing a global service design programme for Coca-Cola Global Business Services. He shares a passion for creativity, user experience, visual design and digital technologies, along with expertise in web strategy, service design and digital content production. Michal works at the intersection of design thinking and digital project management, integrating expertise beyond traditional project management methodology in order to guide idea creation, problem-solving, customer experience design and project execution in delivering business value and customer-centric solutions.

Gabriele Tempesta graduated *cum laude* in Product Design from Politecnico di Milano, with a thesis on a modular self-service platform designed to make abandoned urban areas attractive for the 'wandering citizen'. The thesis was part of the university's '100 Virtuous Cities' research, whose outcomes, including this thesis, were featured at the Italian Pavilion during the 2010 expo. In 2011, he worked as a product design intern at Yang Design, developing concepts for an energy-saving power strip for office environments. He obtained a master's degree in industrial design at Eindhoven University of Technology (TU/e), with a focus on intelligent systems. His graduation work consisted of an awareness system aimed at encouraging students to save energy in the TU/e chemistry department; the largest energy hog on campus. From 2014 onwards, he has been working as the Strategy and Service Design consultant for the Yang Design City Innovation Department; a team dedicated to making Chinese cities better through smart and human-centred design. His work also includes the design of an educational playground for THE One Foundation NGO, and a trend research report on city furniture in the smart city era.

Heikki Tikkanen works as a designer and uses video and audio material to provide service design for businesses. His area of expertise is audio-visual media culture.

Kirsikka Vaajakallio (Ph.D. in design) is the Lead Service Designer, Head of Employee Experience and partner at the service design agency Hellon, which creates unique customer experiences, and helps organisations transform towards customer-centricity by applying an empathic design approach.

Katarina Wetter Edman (Ph.D. in Design, and MFA in Industrial Design, HDK-School of Design and Crafts, Gothenburg University) is a senior lecturer in Service Design at Konstfack University College of Arts, Crafts and Design, Stockholm, Sweden, and a researcher at ExperioLab, County Council of Värmland, Sweden. She has ten years of practical experience in industrial design and design management. Her research focuses on articulation of the emerging field of service design, including service design practice. More specifically, she is interested in the potential contribution of design practice and user involvement through design, or how a specific design competence may be formulated through a pragmatic understanding of inquiry and aesthetics. She is also interested in the role of service design in the public sector.

Erik Widmark has a Master of Fine Arts from Konstfack University College of Arts, Craft and Design in Stockholm, Sweden. With a lifelong curiosity about people and the systems that surround us, Erik has used his industrial design education to develop service design processes and tools. For several years, Erik worked as the service design director for one of Sweden's largest service design agencies. As head of the design department, he was in charge of recruiting, teaching and mentoring his fellow co-workers as well as further developing service design offerings and methods. Over the last few years, Erik has led and coached over 100 service design projects in both the private sector (e.g. banking, insurance and telecom) and the public sector (e.g. public transport, social insurance, public employment and health care). Together with Susanna Nissar, Erik recently started the social innovation agency Expedition Mondial as a way to further explore the boundaries of service design.

Part I

Introduction to industrial service design

What is industrial service design?

1   Introduction to industrial service design

Satu Miettinen

Keywords: industrial service design, the role of designer, outside in, customer-centricity, design for change, employee experience, design for business, industrial service design process

The goal of this chapter is to introduce industrial service design. The making of the book has been an interesting process; the company case studies and the voices of the authors engaged with industry have had a central role. In the book, industrial service design cases present companies like ABB, Autodesk, Bittium, the Coca-Cola Company, L'Oreal, Tetra Pak, Volkswagen, as well as global service design agencies such as Designthinkers, Hellon, Palmu and Veryday. Well-established researchers on service design have contributed their research findings to the book.

The company cases and authors, both from the industry and academia, highlight current themes for industrial service design. They discuss the role of service designers, both in an industrial company, as well as from a consultancy point of view. Human-centred design, or human-centricity, is one of the central themes, along with service design for business. This introductory chapter picks up the themes and formulates the landscape of industrial service design. The chapter also follows up on the industrial service design process to highlight some practical aspects when applying service design in an industrial context.

The content of the book is divided into four parts: Introduction to Industrial Service Design; Industrial Service Design in Practice; Hands-on Industrial Service Design; and Tools for Industrial Service Design. Part I explains the basics of industrial service design. Part II presents and analyses practical service design cases with companies, as well as academic research findings around the methodologies and themes related to the cases. In Part III, experienced designers share their insights and findings related to the work they have been involved with in industrial companies. Part IV is about sharing tools for industrial service design.

While working on the book, it has become clear that industrial service design faces challenges. Many technology-driven companies are confronting a situation where a competitive advantage is gained based on a good customer-service experience. Industrial service designers are challenged to facilitate cultural and behavioural transformations in technology and engineering-orientated companies, which are changing from technical to human-centred thinking. Industrial companies are required to match production speed with market changes and the changing behaviour of customers. Communication and collaboration within large companies has become difficult. Companies have silos, and departments have individual budgets and strategies, which may conflict. It is hard to manage quality when dealing with the issue of outsourcing from a number of companies. For industrial service designers, this means considerable redesign work to accommodate new technologies, strategies and partners. Effective industrial service design can respond to these challenges.

This chapter discusses the findings and conclusions of the authors, and highlights some of the central themes that are relevant to industrial service design.

Service design

The aim of service design is to create customer- or human-centred solutions that make the service experience feel logical, desired, competitive and unique for the user, and boost innovation and engagement in companies and institutions while developing and delivering services. Services have become multi-channel. They are experienced and consumed in person, online or in interactions with robots, as in autonomous driving.

Service design connects the use of different practical design and design research methods, design thinking and various visualisation techniques, linking them with different stakeholders' views during the service design process. Service design is about concretising abstract content into something that can be easily shared, understood, discussed and prototyped together. It is about doing, making and learning through practice. Service design encourages trying and failing early. Focusing on the iterative cycle of engaging users, using mock-ups and cheap prototypes, and evaluating the results in a development process, will result in customer-driven and usable service solutions.

Facilitation has a central role in service design. Designers work as coordinators between all the stakeholders in service-development projects, acting as overall choreographers of the service experience. Service design follows core principles like human-centredness and co-design, creating empathy (Postma et al. 2012), an iterative process with a great deal of prototyping (Blomkvist 2014; Miettinen et al. 2012), using and developing innovative design tools and methods (Løvlie et al. 2013; Miettinen and Koivisto 2009; Stickdorn and Schneider 2012), facilitation and peer-to-peer and practice-based learning (Kuure and Miettinen 2013) that guide the service-development process.

Service design is a new approach for developing services that are immaterial and abstract. Digitalisation affects user experiences and the ways in which experiences are consumed and enjoyed. A good film creates good feelings and memories, but the experience itself is consumed at the same time that it is experienced. Moreover, the ways in which a film can be experienced have changed in the digital economy era. Films can be viewed not only in a cinema but also on mobile devices such as iPads, both on the go and at home. Films are often obtained online through Netflix or from another service provider rather than rented from video/DVD rental shops. Business models have changed, and this is particularly true for services. Service design provides the design tools and methods to analyse and develop the service experience in a holistic and human-centred way. It also helps to concretise and visualise complex processes and ecosystems. However, service design and management are challenging since services are multi-channel. They are delivered in person and through mobile and digital channels. The aim of service design is to coordinate all these and make them understandable to the user.

Service design is an academic discipline (for example, Meroni and Sangiorgi 2011; Miettinen and Valtonen 2013), and has roots in design research, especially in the areas of empathic and participatory design. The other side of service design is a strong practice (see Løvlie et al. 2013; Stickdorn and Schneider 2012) with service design consultancies in companies. This book focuses on the practical side of service design, highlighting various industrial service design cases that illustrate how service design is applied. Companies and consultancies are developing new methods and applying service design in the development of services in a number of business areas, from software and hardware production and development to health care and hospitality. A significant portion of service design research is applied and based on case-study research or action research with companies or public institutions.

Role and work of an industrial service designer

The role of a designer has been scrutinised and researched for decades, both from design research and engineering points of view (Bayazit 2004). One of the main research focuses has been on how designers work and the organisation of the design process itself. Nowadays, the research focus has shifted to the role of design in the innovation process (Deserti and Rizzo 2014). A designer's role now includes more research skills and tools, especially when the role of service design is discussed.

Service design is not only an operational activity where user insights are collected and new service concepts are produced. Service designers should have a role at the beginning of the process when strategic decisions are made (Wetter Edman 2013). This will facilitate the whole service design process and improve the understanding of projects, goals and outcomes. In industrial companies, it is important to engage in design and design thinking (Brown 2009) across a wide spectrum of design areas: service design, user experience (UX) design and product design. Often, service designers work with UX design or, conversely, UX designers work with service design.

There is still a lot of work to do to create awareness of service design and the use of this approach in the industrial context. This boils down to a service designer working to promote service design or design thinking across the organisation. The service designer thus helps to foster a deep understanding on the part of users, and improves functionality across the organisation, as well as partnering different sections. A service designer can promote user needs and find opportunities within those needs (Wetter Edman 2014). The role of a service designer is especially important in business-to-business service development, where the end-user's needs are crucial but nobody is directly representing them. Service designers understand the pulse of industry and utilise this understanding in their work.

Changes in the current economy and business models have influenced both the role of design and the role of service designers. Design has expanded from concrete artefacts to abstract, social and digital content. One of the main activities that service designers are involved with is co-design with stakeholders. Service designers work with stakeholders (and especially users) to co-develop services using innovative tools and methods that often involve workshops (Sanders and Stappers 2008). The role of service design is constructed around the social context of designing for services. Thus, a service designer works as a facilitator, listening to people and trying to understand and learn from them (Steen et al. 2011). A service designer collects partial solutions and enables and encourages people to come up with more complete solutions. Co-design and workshops require considerable preparation and tools. Often, the methods and processes must be customised to fit the needs of the development process and the goals of the future service. In co-design and workshop processes, it is essential that the right people are recruited to participate and that everyone knows the purpose and mission of a particular workshop.

Customer-centric companies are looking outside in

Industries are branding and developing service quality and customer experience, as well as developing online-to-offline services. All these activities are focused on customer-centricity. The core of service design is human-centred thinking. Service design offers companies a new way to look at both their service development and service delivery processes (Kimbell 2009). In service design, both service development and service delivery are constructed around the user and their customer experience (CX). In practice, this means that the customer's journeys are identified and create a flux: logical, enjoyable and memorable experiences that lead to recommendations and return.

The outside-in perspective means that a service designer uses service design tools to map the UX and its service opportunities, disseminating end-user motivations and journeys, including touchpoints and 'as-is' pathways, to corporations. This kind of outside-in service design (Bates and Davis 2009) requires taking a step outside the traditional method of designing a service around an existing process, and looking at the service offering from an outside perspective. Industrial service designers need to find new service opportunities and ways to create more competitive service experiences. Service design offers a number of tools to both analyse and reconstruct the customer journey (Miettinen and Koivisto 2009), such as service blueprinting, which involves analysing different phases and service delivery channels and structures, including employee activities, as well as customer activities and emotions during the service journey. Tools include the creation of personas, which describe the users' characteristics and needs and the everyday context for service development, identifying service touchpoints through which the service is enjoyed and experienced. Creating an improved customer experience is one of the main goals of service design (Zomerdijk and Voss 2010). In industrial companies, service design tools are applied not only for recreational users but increasingly for professional users: doctors, nurses, maintenance staff and technicians. The professional user experience needs to be applied when using persona or blueprinting tools.

In practice, customer-centricity is constructed using service design tools. In this book, Veryday shares a Tetra Pak case study in which Veryday was given an opportunity to work around silos and create a service concept horizontally across the value chain, for markets in China and Brazil. Large amounts of customer insights were collected to create a credible data pool. The data were processed further to create value propositions. Tools such as video, scenarios and opportunity mapping were used in the process. In service design, co-design sessions typically occur during the design process. In the sessions, materials are both abstract and tangible: talking and doing. Many discussions take place during the co-design sessions, which materialise in Post-It stickers, notes, paper prototypes and experience prototypes. The storytelling and narrative method is central for creating understanding and insight. The stories and narratives construct a bridge between the customer and the service provider. Materials and documentation from co-design sessions carry a lot of meaning that is then interpreted. The interpretation process is important, and must be connected with value creation and business-case concept production and/or development. Notes and materials should be interpreted in a way such that business or value-creation opportunities are recognised in concrete ways; for example, locating or categorising materials and interpretations within these recognised opportunities. These opportunities can be created around the establishment or understanding of necessary service characteristics or ways of organising service production and delivery.

In industrial service design, it is crucial to ensure that an organisation is customer-centric at a practical level, not only in its white papers. Service design consultancies like Palmu encourage companies to think and talk about customers. To value customers, it is necessary to meet with them, and there should be spontaneous product testing and development in collaboration with customers. Customer-centricity is not only something that is visible to the customer; it is the core structure by which services are produced and delivered to customers (Teixeira et al. 2012). When a company is truly customer-centric, customer values drive the service-development process. As a concrete example described in the book of applying customer-centricity, ABB established a CUX (customer user experience) programme to support a change towards customer-centric actions and customer-centred thinking at ABB.

Designing for change and employee experience

Transformation and change are always discussed and implicitly present in industrial service design. The goal of the service design process is to create opportunities, develop and improve. Service design is an active process that creates pressure for organisational structures and processes; it is transformation design (Sangiorgi 2011). Transformation design and transformational change are discussed more in relation to social innovation (Cottam and Leadbeater 2004; Parker and Heapy 2006), but they are paramount in the modern era of newly emerging business models and collaborative business. New service solutions may require organisational changes in processes and in ways of working. Service design needs to have tools and methods for facilitating change and committing people to these change processes.

Service design is often about developing a new company culture where people are engaged in creating new solutions through service design. In this kind of company culture, it is important to understand each other, and good self-awareness is necessary to understand another person. Designing for change is always a challenge. There has to be a strategy and strong inclusion of the staff to be successful. Design can be used as a collaborative method in the change process (Brandt and Messeter 2004). Implementing change is about making people show their ideas, creating ownership, providing more choices and commitment and offering challenges. In organisations, changes are taking place, but often the process is slow and requires patience and the gathering of like-minded followers.

Service design is not only focused on CX; it is a holistic activity in which the people experiencing and delivering the service are equally important. To deliver great service experience and quality, the work has to be meaningful.

Work should be taken in a more experiential direction. Human-resource management faces new challenges, with millennials becoming an increasingly large part of the workforce and many generations working side by side.

Service design is a new tool that can be used to improve the employee experience and increase digitalisation, which is part of service production and delivery, as well as CX. Service design offers tools such as employee experience journey mapping, which is described in this book. Such mapping helps to redesign and develop scenarios and analyse the existing experience to better understand the holistic and complex employee experience.

Service designing business

It is critical for every business to understand the customer's world and ideal values. In service design, this understanding is created through an understanding of the cultural context and the system of values and meanings. Service design tools are used to create in-depth insights that can be analysed and used to create value propositions that respond to customers' needs in a concrete way. Value is created by helping the customer to achieve their goals. Service propositions are often based on interaction and coproduction with customers. To create a viable service product, it is necessary to not only communicate with the customer but also to have a dialogue and hear what the customer has to say. A viable service product must be based on customers' and stakeholders' knowledge, skills and activities. Service designers need to create business opportunities and revenue around users' profiles and behavioural patterns. As service systems are becoming more complex, it is no longer enough to simply profile the user; rather, the profile must be created around the greater business ecosystem, including the stakeholders.

Service design enables organisations to design and deliver value propositions (Osterwalder et al. 2015), helping organisations to overcome challenges that prevent the creation of meaningful and innovative value propositions. Service design helps in understanding the prejudices and the historical and development contexts of organisations. Human-centred design and recognising opportunities is not enough. The service design process should result in cost savings and additional revenues, as industrial service design aims for growth. Service design should also increase customer loyalty, lead to the discovery of new unique selling points, result in higher margins and speed up the innovation process.

Service design contributes to achieving business goals by understanding customers' value-creation processes. Design practice, which refers to the use of service design tools and expertise to gather and interpret data and relate it to business goals, resulting in service concepts and scenarios, responds to this need. Designers create an understanding of the service experience and service context, and are able to analyse users' participation in the service process. They create an understanding of the value in use (Sandström et al. 2008) and the value in context (Chandler and Vargo 2011) for the customers. Service-dominant logic explains how things, people and systems interact, and as a result the relations, experiences, knowledge and contexts become important for the customer while creating value (Vargo and Lusch 2004). The locus of value creation can be in the customer sphere, the provider sphere or the joint sphere (Grönroos 2008).

Service design can be used to define a minimum viable product (Moogk 2012). Service design methodology contributes to developing a product through a series of experiments. Service designers scan the market to find user prototypes and work to define unique selling points. Service design creates value by constructing a service concept that describes opportunities discovered from user insights. It utilises narratives that include trends, insights from users/customer stories and business-case findings, which are based on evaluations from business teams. Service designers produce impact scenarios that are based on credible quantitative and user data. Service designers understand trends, such as cloud technologies, which have caused business models to shift away from subscriptions and towards licencing; new markets in which industry reseller relationships might be closer than the end-user relationship.

Industrial service design process

The industrial service design process has to be embedded into existing corporate structures and processes. The role of a service designer is to negotiate and initiate service design within these structures and find spaces where service design thinking can be used. We live in an era of digitalisation and rapid change. Companies that are unable to institute more agile processes may find it difficult to remain abreast of market changes.

The double diamond model of the Design Council (2007), which describes the four phases of the development process – discover (initial idea, user needs); define (interpretation, business objectives); develop (solution development, prototyping and evaluation); and deliver (final testing and launch) – has proven to be very useful in service design and has been well adopted (Stickdorn and Schwarzenberger 2016). Many service design companies describe their service design processes as including the principles of 'the IDEO way' (Kelley 2007). For 'the IDEO way', it is important to have an in-depth understanding of the users' context, involving teams in the development process and early prototyping. Van Oosterom (2009) from Designthinkers proposes a five-phase service design process that consists of discovering, conceptualising, designing, building and implementing. This is similar to Engine's (2009) three phases: identify, build and measure. All these processes support the idea of discovering and understanding the user, using this information in business development and delivering something new to the market, all of which are cornerstones of the double diamond model. In industrial service design, this double diamond process is often integrated into running a pilot phase.

1. Pre-process: strategic design thinking and internal marketing

For many industrial service designers, the service design process does not begin with a brief or in-depth understanding of customers, but rather with preparing the company and its product and service development for the service design process. This phase requires marketing activities inside the company to find key partners who might participate in the case. This kind of internal marketing is necessary to create partnerships inside the company and identify potential development areas.

Early strategic alignment is needed inside the company. Industrial service designers are familiar with strategic design thinking. Thus, service designers should be included in strategic discussions within the company to ensure the inclusion of this thinking in the company's processes and eventual structure. Service design tools can be used to position the company. It is critical to understand where the company is and where it wants to go. Without this understanding, it is impossible to choose the right tools or find the right partnerships. Furthermore, it is important to maximise the innovation potential of the company. There should be a balanced mix of people with different profiles and personalities. Group equality and autonomy are important to make good decisions. A hierarchical system can easily destroy agility and prototyping mentality. Information should also be provided regarding the resources that are available for the project.

2. Running a pilot with a team

Industrial service design is about practical activities that are included in company processes through different sections. The typical way to initiate service design is through pilots, where staff and especially middle management are recruited to participate. When running a pilot, it is helpful to go back to the strategic level and include an initial strategic alignment workshop in the project to ensure that the pilot has the right direction and is in line with the company's strategy.

Industrial service design is a team effort. Pilots encourage people from different business units to participate. A service designer's practical responsibility is to aid the innovation process inside the company. This includes, for example, facilitating practical empathy to obtain and spread user insights and understanding throughout the organisation, as well as using visualisation techniques to communicate and concretise user insights, research data or service concepts. Workflow and management can be organised around an agile process with sprints (Stellman and Greene 2014). This helps scale up the process through a large organisation while still keeping it innovative.

Collaboration with teams inside the organisation occurs by utilising a service design framework; that is, understanding the user and mapping the service experience. Preparing a service pilot can include running a beta version of a service and selecting testers. Pilots can be based on a prototype that has been deconstructed to discover features for testing, and obtain feedback to create a detailed stakeholder map to learn more about the value chain and network. The prototype can provide information for quantitative studies for creating business scenarios. In addition, prototypes can help in developing criteria for testing candidates. Once the beta version of the service is running, other methods are used to gather user insights. Some of these insights can be shared immediately. For instance, video can be used as a tool, creating podcasts from customers' concepts and sharing them right away. Insights can be analysed using opportunity mapping by crashing all the insights into a visible format in a large paper, as Veryday did.

Pilots always involve the use of business model design tools, such as the service logic business model canvas. Business design tools help a company to determine how to reach a single customer using a customer journey map, the whole organisation through a service map and multiple stakeholders – as well as how the organisation's offerings meet customer needs. Multidisciplinary work with financial experts strengthens the viability of the service concept. The pilot should result in a business-case and scenario analysis, increase information about requirements for the proposed service and contribute to the strategic vision for new opportunities. When conducting a pilot, it is important to disseminate the results and use them in internal marketing to validate the effectiveness of the service design.

3. Scale up

When designing at a particular scale, business units and service providers play an important role, and so they must have a good communication and effective co-design process. There should be a strong inside-out perspective that is focused on developing a dialogue to respond to user needs and transfer those needs into service specifications, and then further into user journeys and enjoyable touchpoints for the users (Patrício et al. 2011). Industrial service designers must see the bigger picture and include user needs into a larger journey view. Moreover, service designers need to move away from designing one action and consider the whole process. A sequence of well-designed actions will lead to a unified service experience. The customer experience framework allows zooming in and out of customer experiences from touchpoints into the systems.

The challenge of scaling is always present in the industrial service design process. The complexity of service design projects has increased, with the projects including multiple stakeholders inside and outside an organisation. The customer perspective needs to meet the organisational structure and strategy. In the public sector, the customer perspective should be discussed in terms of multi-organisation offerings and creating a good service experience for customers. In many cases, users move horizontally while service providers move vertically in their own silos. This causes hiccups and bottlenecks in the service experience from the customer's point of view. Collaboration is needed to realise inside-out thinking, which motivates employees, and an outside-in approach to share customers' view of the organisation.

Designing for transformational change (Chapman 2002) is about scaling up service design inside the company and acting on strategic alignment. Service design can facilitate this transformational change (Nutt and Backoff 1997). Many co-design methods can enable the dialogue and behavioural changes needed to change thinking and working patterns. It is often essential to discover change agents in the organisation to aid in this transformation process. Scaling up requires an action plan to concretise the steps necessary to make changes.

Conclusion

It is clear that the era of service design and industrial service design has just begun. During the past twenty years, industry has learned to utilise design thinking and human-centred design and to find new business opportunities by contextualising and analysing user information. As described by designers in the book, there are still challenges with regard to transforming company culture towards a more holistic and cultural approach when developing new services.

Service design offers a new kind of thinking and tools for responding to rapidly changing business environments. New innovations and service business models are developed within innovation ecosystems such as Silicon Valley. Service design can offer methodologies for creating partnerships and participating in dialogues with users, helping companies to transform and discover new business opportunities,

References

Bates, P. and Davis, F. (2009) Outside-in service design. *International Journal of Leadership in Public Services*, 5(3), pp. 43–49.

Bayazit, N. (2004) Investigating design: A review of forty years of design research. *Design issues, 20*(1), pp. 16–29.

Blomkvist, J. (2014) Representing future situations of service: Prototyping in service design. Linköping Studies in Arts and Science, No. 618. Linköping University.

Brandt, E. and Messeter, J. (2004, July) Facilitating collaboration through design games. In: *Proceedings of the Eighth Conference on Participatory Design: Artful Integration: Interweaving Media, Materials and Practices, Volume 1* (pp. 121–131). New York: ACM.

Brown, T. (2009) *Change by design. How design thinking transforms organizations and inspires innovation.* New York: HarperCollins.

Chandler, J.D. and Vargo, S.L. (2011) Contextualization and value-in-context: How context frames exchange. *Marketing Theory, 11*(1), pp. 35–49.

Chapman, J.A. (2002) A framework for transformational change in organisations. *Leadership & Organization Development Journal, 23*(1), pp. 16–25.

Cottam, H. and Leadbeater, C. (2004) *RED paper 01: Health: Co-creating services.* London: Design Council.

Deserti, A. and Rizzo, F. (2014) Design and the cultures of enterprises. *Design Issues, 30*(1), pp. 36–56.

Design Council (2007) *Eleven Lessons: Managing Design in Eleven Global Brands. A Study of the Design Process.* London: Design Council. Available at: www.designcouncil.org.uk/sites/default/files/asset/document/ElevenLessons_Design_Council, 20(282), p. 29.

Engine (2009). Engine Group. Retrieved from www.enginegroup.co.uk/ (accessed 6 May 2009).

Grönroos, C. (2008) Service logic revisited: Who creates value? And who co-creates? *European Business Review, 20*(4), pp. 298–314.

Kelley, T. (2007) *The Art of Innovation: Lessons in Creativity from IDEO, America's Leading Design Firm.* New York: Crown Business.

Kimbell, L. (2009) The turn to service design. In: G. Julier and L. Moor (Eds.) *Design and Creativity: Policy, Management and Practice* (pp. 157–173). Oxford, UK: Berg.

Kuure, E. and Miettinen, S. (2013) Learning through action: Introducing the Innovative Simulation and Learning Environment Service Innovation Corner (SINCO). In: *World Conference on E-Learning in Corporate, Government, Healthcare, and Higher Education* (Vol. 2013, No. 1, pp. 1536–1545). Available at www.learntechlib.org/p/115095

Løvlie, L., Polaine, A. and Reason, B. (2013) *Service Design: From Insight to Implementation.* New York: Rosenfield Media.

Meroni, A. and Sangiorgi, D. (2011) *Design for Services,* Aldershot, UK: Gower.

Miettinen, S. and Koivisto, M. (2009) *Designing Services with Innovative Methods,* University of Art and Design. Retrieved from www.ellibs.com/book/9789525018424 (accessed 15 April 2016).

Miettinen, S., Rontti, S., Kuure, E. and Lindström, A. (2012) Realizing design thinking through a service design process and an innovative prototyping laboratory: Introducing service innovation corner (SINCO). DRS 2012, Bangkok Chulalongkorn University, Bangkok, Thailand, 1–4 July 2012. Retrieved from www.designresearchsociety.org/images/publications/2012drs/drs2012_vol2.pdf (accessed 9 June 2016).

Miettinen, S. and Valtonen, A. (2013) *Service Design with Theory: Discussions on Change, Value and Methods.* Rovaniemi: Lapland University Press.

Moogk, D.R. (2012) Minimum viable product and the importance of experimentation in technology startups. *Technology Innovation Management Review, 2*(3), p. 23.

Nutt, P.C. and Backoff, R.W. (1997) Facilitating transformational change. *The Journal of Applied Behavioural Science, 33*(4), pp. 490–508.

Osterwalder, A., Pigneur, Y., Bernarda, G. and Smith, A. (2015) *Value Proposition Design: How to Create Products and Services Customers Want*. Hoboken, NJ: John Wiley.

Parker, S. and Heapy, J. (2006) *The Journey to the Interface*. London: Demos.

Patrício, L., Fisk, R.P. and Constantine, L. (2011) Multilevel service design: From customer value constellation to service experience blueprinting. *Journal of Service Research, 14*(2), pp. 180–200.

Postma, C., Lauche, K. and Stappers, P.J. (2012) Social theory as a thinking tool for empathic design. *Design Issues, 28*(1), pp. 30–49.

Sanders, E.B.N. and Stappers, P.J. (2008) Co-creation and the new landscapes of design. *Co-design, 4*(1), pp. 5-18.

Sandström, S., Edvardsson, B., Kristensson, P. and Magnusson, P. (2008) Value in use through service experience. *Managing Service Quality: An International Journal, 18*(2), pp. 112–126.

Sangiorgi, D. (2011) Transformative services and transformation design. *International Journal of Design, 5*(2), pp. 29-40.

Steen, M., Manschot, M.A.J. and De Koning, N. (2011) Benefits of co-design in service design projects. *International Journal of Design, 5*(2), pp. 53–60.

Stellman, A. and Greene, J. (2014) *Learning Agile: Understanding Scrum, XP, Lean, and Kanban*. Sebastopol, CA: O'Reilly Media Inc.

Stickdorn, M. and Schneider, J. (2012) *This is Service Design Thinking: Basics, Tools, Cases*. Amsterdam: BIS.

Stickdorn, M. and Schwarzenberger, K. (2016) Service design in tourism. In: H. Siller and A. Zehrer (Eds.), *Entrepreneurship und Tourismus: Unternehmerisches Denken und Erfolgskonzepte aus der Praxis* (p. 2261). Vienna: Linde International.

Teixeira, J., Patrício, L., Nunes, N.J., Nóbrega, L., Fisk, R.P. and Constantine, L. (2012) Customer experience modeling: From customer experience to service design. *Journal of Service Management, 23*(3), pp. 362–376.

Van Oosterom, A. (2009) Who do we think we are? In: S. Miettinen (Ed.), *Designing Services with Innovative Methods* (pp. 162–179). Helsinki: University of Art and Design.

Vargo, S.L. and Lusch, R.F. (2004) Evolving to a new dominant logic for marketing. *Journal of Marketing, 68*(1), pp. 1–17.

Wetter Edman, K. (2013) Relations and rationales of user's involvement in service design and service management. In: S. Miettinen and A. Valtonen (Eds.), *Service Design with Theory. Discussions on Change, Value and Methods* (pp. 105–114). Rovaniemi: Lapland University Press.

Wetter Edman, K. (2014) Design for service: A framework for articulating designers' contribution as interpreter of users' experience. ArtMonitor Doctoral Dissertations and Licentiate Theses, No, 45. Sweden: University of Gothenburg.

Zomerdijk, L.G. and Voss, C.A. (2010) Service design for experience-centric services. *Journal of Service Research, 13*(1), pp. 67–82.

Part II

Industrial service design in practice

Sharing industrial service design
case studies

2 Customer experience and service employee experience

Two sides of the same coin

Kirsikka Vaajakallio, Tuuli Mattelmäki, Virpi Roto and Yichen Lu

Keywords: Hellon, employee experience, customer experience, Active@work

Service is constructed of relationships, interactions and cocreation. To function well, both front-stage and backstage processes and experiences need to be addressed. While the emphasis in service design has been on user and customer experience, this chapter opens a discussion on the role of service employee experience as a growing interest in service design. This chapter aims to address the topic by introducing the authors' reflections and experiences on the topic. Rather than a conclusion, this is an invitation to a discussion and further research on the interplay of employee and customer experiences at face-to-face service touchpoints.

Expanding the focus from users and customers to employees' experience

Service design emphasises human-centredness as the starting point and customer experiences as the aim. According to Saco and Goncalves, '(service design is) a human-centred approach that focuses on customer experience and the quality of service encounter as the key value for success' (2008: 12). Service design is also a holistic approach that looks at both sides of the service: customers' experiences and service producers' processes. In the former, the focus is largely on individuals' emotional experiences, whereas the latter focuses mainly on technical systems, processes and tools, and easily oversees individual service employees and their experiences.

In those cases where employee experience is of interest, it is typically handled separately from designing for customer experiences, although similar processes and methods can be applied to both. To give an example, approximately ten years ago, Mattelmäki and Vaajakallio (*née* Lehtonen) worked as design researchers in a project that applied user-centred design methods to understand ageing workers' well-being at work. In that project, user experience, empathy and co-design were the key words when human-centred design competence was first extended to look at social and organisational topics. The Active@ work project aimed to design alternative arrangements for ageing employees and addressed the global challenge of employees getting older and retiring, resulting in organisations losing critical competence and tacit knowledge (Mattelmäki and Lehtonen 2006).

The project started by considering the issues that motivated workers to remain at work and what triggered early retirement. The ageing workers were invited to discussions where they documented and reflected upon their everyday experiences, recorded their motivations and challenges, shared stories and envisioned ideas for alternative arrangements. Initially, the design researchers – who focused mainly on empathic design and design for user experience and related methods – were not on solid ground. However, they were able to regain their confidence quickly during the process. In addition, taking user experience as a starting point and utilising human-centred and co-design methods was fruitful for addressing working life challenges. The ageing workers were employees in an organisation offering catering, cleaning and maintenance services to State schools. Although school maintenance or cleaning is not necessarily the focus of attention when things work well, it quickly becomes an issue when it does not.

At that time, the Active@work project was considered explorative in the way it utilised design methods to understand and design for employee experience. The project ensured that the design approach was applicable for investigating and designing for the employee experience and generating insights related to meaningful work: motivations, frustrations, hopes and dislikes, as well as ergonomics, leadership and power issues. Recently, a similar approach has been suggested to translate typical user-centred design (UCD) principles for organisational design by Gruber et al. (2015), who also highlight the need to focus on employee experiences, not just workflows and tools, and to consider the application of collaborative engagement, as well as the emotional nature of experiences. In the Active@work project, the focus was on the employee experience only. However, one of the weaknesses of the project was that the researchers studied and designed for ageing workers' work experience separately from customer experience, although it had already been acknowledged that they are connected. Considering both at the same time would have resulted in a bigger impact for the business, as suggested by Gruber et al., 'enabling the employee to understand how their role (and associated actions) contributes value to the organisation's goals, and how it creates new value for its customers' (2015, p. 4).

Customer and employee experience: two sides of the same service experience

Vaajakallio's recent experiences working as one of the leading service designers at Hellon, a design agency specialising in service and transformation design, and her role as Head of Employee Experience have highlighted the need for creating a balance between customer and employee experience in service encounters; without the latter, the first does not exist. Based on her insights, both in internal discussions at the company and with her clients in particular, in most service organisations a big part of the meaningful work experience comes from the ability to provide a service that is valued highly by customers. Who would not like to hear positive feedback and kind words about the way they have performed? The challenge, however, is not having a realistic image of customers' needs, desires and fears, which influence the service experience. Without knowledge of what actually matters and brings value, it is hard to meet expectations. Incorrect assumptions regarding customers' wishes are often made.

To tackle this issue, Vaajakallio has started to explore 'empathy videos' as a powerful tool in diverse organisations. Empathy videos are short stories of customers that illustrate their daily lives when using the service. These videos provide contextual insights and faces to the experiences, and help service staff to empathise with the customers' perspective. Empathic videos are used in many ways: for example, to share customer understanding; brainstorm new methods for interaction; support and delight the persons in the videos; or as a part of training. Enabling employees to have a more empathic view of their customers reflects changes within the management domain, from operational effectiveness towards understanding and designing for customer and employee journeys and experiences (Gruber et al. 2015).

In service design, getting positive feedback from customers is often one of the underlying design targets. Thus, Saco and Goncalves (2008) suggest that in order to design great customer experiences, companies need to focus on selecting talented frontline personnel and staff that have genuine skills and motivation to serve customers. However, the experience is typically evaluated from a business success point of view only, focusing on net promoter scores or public feedback on social media. We believe that the customer experience is more than just numbers. It is a meaningful factor influencing why many people do the work they do. However, it is challenging to find service employees who interact with their customers daily, and who understand and admit that they do not necessarily have a correct view of what actually matters to their customers. In this regard, empathic videos may be a useful tool. It is also important to recognise the reasons behind the wrong assumptions that service employees may have.

If we do not understand employee experience, it is hard to consider the impact of improving, modifying and introducing new services from customers' point of view. Hence, it is important to ensure that we create solutions that are not only good for customers, but also meet frontline personnel needs and expectations. If the solution is not meaningful for the personnel, it will be unable to fulfil promises to the customers. In order to co-create meaningful service experiences, all the components of the service co-creation should be addressed. Employee experience is shaped in the same way that customer experience is shaped – by expectations, motivations, desires and fears – and hence it deserves similar attention.

One of Vaajakallio's examples comes from a project in which her company worked to improve the customer experience in personal and business banking. Customer insights, which addressed customers' satisfaction with their personal finance adviser and the need to be able to trust their advice and the bank as a whole, were used to create an entirely new service model and servicescape (e.g. the way in which customers are welcomed, round tables for meetings and a home-like atmosphere). In that project, the designers were not able to conduct an in-depth study of employee experience (the marketing department and bank manager had been more involved), but they were aware that some of the employees criticised the new model before they had any experience with it. The criticisms were caused by the changes demanded of the employees. For example, there were no longer any individual meeting rooms and everyone was required to welcome customers at the door. Since negative emotions were identified, it was suggested to the bank management that designers should be allowed to organise a creative workshop for the employees to practise the new model, thus tackling some of the fears collaboratively.

A workshop with the employees was held soon after the opening of the new branch. In the workshop, the employees were encouraged to share tricks, best practices and other positive things with each other, as well as ideas about how they could modify the model to better meet their daily needs without risking the customer experience. The creative workshop helped to present the new practices in a more positive light. However, it was only after customers praised the change that the employees' attitude to the novel solution improved. Similar cases have recently been observed in several other fields. To ensure successful implementation of new service practices, it is important to involve employees in the design of new practices, share best practices and ensure understanding of the value that the new actions bring to their customers.

To bring customer and employee experiences closer to each other in the banking case, the interior was designed as an enabling platform to meet customers' needs. For example, a round table made service moments feel like the parties were on the same side, eliciting trust among customers, and small tablet computers were introduced as a shared display for customers and employees. Along with home-like decorations, materials and colours, these changes brought people closer to each other while minimising the perception of opposite interests – a negative emotion customers had felt previously. In addition to collaborative workshops and customer understanding, designing tools for the employees that promoted a service style preferred by the customers supported employees to change their behaviour and adopt new practices.

The employee experience is even more important in industrial services because there are fewer relationships between service providers and clients in business-to-business (B2B) domains, and thus they are more important. Industrial services are also often related to large, expensive systems with a relatively long life span, which means that the relationships are much longer than in consumer services.

Lu and Roto, who are also authors of this article, worked in a five-year Fimecc User Experience and Usability in Complex Systems (UXUS) research programme[1] that studied experiences in the Finnish metal and engineering industries. During the programme, it became clear that industrial services between two companies are not restricted to the services that a company sells to the client, but rather take place in many phases of customer relations and the product lifecycle: services for finding the right product, for sales negotiations, delivery, installation, maintenance and for planning renewal. These touchpoints are part of the customer journey and influence the customer experience. Much could be done to improve both the customer and employee experiences at these touchpoints, and all employees acting in the touchpoints, such as salesmen, should be seen as service providers.

Lu and Roto's research focuses on experience design. This design process starts with defining experience goals towards which the designers strive. Lu and Roto (2015) found that experiential aspects are hardly ever taken as a starting point when designing tools that people use at work. Instead, the requirements include pragmatic aspects such as ergonomics, cognition, security or performance improvement. To test how experience design can be used in B2B industrial domains, they organised an Experience-driven Design course at Aalto University in Finland. The student assignments came from UXUS partner companies from the domain of heavy industry.

In the following we introduce two student cases that emphasised employees' experience in the B2B metal industry. The first design case was a user experience (UX) playroom, which is a multifunctional space for customer involvement in different phases of business collaboration. The room is used by engineers, salesmen and anyone who is able to improve user and customer experiences. The students started to consider how to evoke an experience of pride for the salesmen when sales demonstrations were performed for customers in the UX playroom, how to inspire the engineers in problem-solving when performing usability tests with the end users in the room, and how to motivate different stakeholders to envision the future of the product in the UX playroom. Eventually, the UX playroom concept was developed to foster organisational awareness of the latent impact of human-to-human interaction in long-term customer relationships in the business-to-business (B2B) industry.[2]

In the other case, the students were asked to design a portable tool for a salesman to demonstrate a tugboat steering system with an existing simulation application for customers. The students began by envisioning a salesman as Q, the fictional head of 'gadgetry' in the British Secret Service, who builds sophisticated devices for James Bond and other agents. Since metal industry customers are also interested in technology, they might enjoy being served like Secret Service agents. The image of Q guided ideation for a salesman's experience in customer meetings to show their expertise in product demonstration and instil organisational pride in their work. The final experience scenario imagined the salesman driving to the presentation stage with an impressive vehicle, such as a Segway embedded with boat-steering controls. The steering system was demonstrated through a vivid and novel presentation, similar to how Q demonstrates the functionalities of devices to 007.[3]

The above case examples considered the service touchpoint design by emphasising the employees' perspective, as well as the customer's perspective. We suggest that a combination of service and experience design is a fruitful approach for designing interaction experiences, both for service employees and customers. To expand the focus beyond customers' experiences, service blueprints could be complemented with ones that highlight employees' experiences (Figure 2.1).

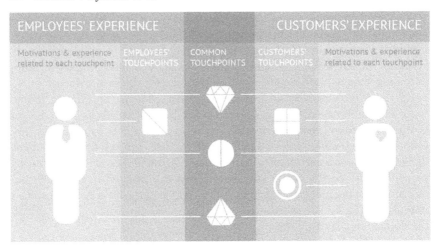

Figure 2.1 Designing for touchpoint interaction: extending the focus to service employees' experience.

Bitner et al. state that 'all parts of the organization should be focused on the common goal of creating an integrated, memorable and favourable customer experience' (2008: 4). This is because 'meaningful customer experiences and the resulting emotional bonds are more important than rational motivations in creating customer loyalty' (ibid.). In service design, this typically requires designing different touchpoints that influence a customer's experience in the front-stage and backstage systems and processes related to them. Frontline employees are burdened with demands on how they should behave and perform to keep customers happy, although the best customer service in face-to-face services often results from employees who enjoy and are motivated by their work. Our view is that when employees are supported by tools, processes and facilities that increase their motivation to work, customer experience is improved. This is why service design should shift its attention from customer experience to designing *touchpoint interaction* (i.e. the points at which people – customers and service employees – meet and co-create services). See Figure 2.2.

Based on our experiences, we have recognised two main challenges when designing with both sides of the coin in mind. First, the holistic experience design perspective challenges organisational silos by emphasising that understanding, developing and delivering a great customer experience is a cross-functional activity. Internal power relations, responsibilities and separate budgets will be challenged when customer experience and employee experience are developed together. This challenge is due to the traditional distinction between home bases and responsibilities in organisations. Second, as discussed by Matveinen et al. (2015), service design projects are often initiated at the service encounter level. When working at this level, service design projects focus on creating service concepts that will enhance the customer experience. Project owners on this level typically exclude systemic influences such as employees'

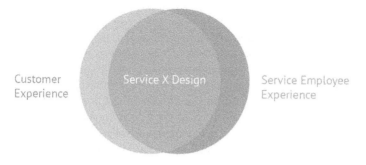

Customer
Experience

Service X Design

Service Employee
Experience

Figure 2.2 Service designers should design for experiences addressing both sides of the coin.

roles, processes and education – all of which are at the heart of employee experience – and factors that also have a huge impact on the customer experience. To overcome these two challenges, the support and engagement of top management is necessary. Increasing the awareness of top managers of design opportunities to improve business, by addressing more empathic and soft values both internally and outwardly, is an important topic for further consideration.

For those who want to increase the understanding of top management and establish service and employee experience design in the organisation, we suggest the following based on the lessons learnt from our cases:

- Gather examples and proofs of concept from successful case examples that also include numeric data and business impact (see, e.g., Gruber et al. 2015). Share them in the form of stories and narratives to evoke emotional responses and support their memorisation. Organise creative top management workshops for going through the examples about service design cases.
- Involve all internal stakeholders who have something at stake with regard to customer experience or employee experience from the beginning – from setting appropriate goals to co-designing new solutions. It may be difficult to organise everyone's schedules, but the effort is worthwhile. Consider how to make every event effective and inspirational: emphasise customer voice as a common ground – few people will deny the importance of customer experience since satisfied customers are crucial if a company is to survive in the long term. Be aware of the design readiness and capabilities of the organisation, applying methods and processes accordingly.
- Invest in internal communication to support a mindset change. The creation of empathic, high-quality videos and other narratives requires resources, but if they are well designed, they can be utilised on several occasions and for varied purposes (also publicly).
- Identify and assign customer and employee experience ambassadors throughout the organisation. These should be individuals who find the service design approach more natural and inspiring than others do. Provide education, peer support and tools for the motivated individuals to become spokespersons and start practising new ways of doing.

Conclusion

We have identified a new trend in service design that pays attention not only to the customer/user experience but also to the employee experience. From holistic experience design and service design perspectives, we have addressed the need to bring the customer experience and the employee experience closer to each other by viewing them as two sides of the same coin. The motivation for raising the discussion on employee experience is to shed light on the potential we see in designing for customer and employee experience holistically, instead of treating them separately. This is very meaningful when supporting organisations to move towards a more customer-centred mindset and way of working.

One of the reasons for increasing attention on the employee experience is to attract the best employees and meet the expectations of Generation Y employees (Gruber et al. 2015). When looking at the employee experience holistically, it is necessary to include people management and organisational culture. For future studies and further discussion, we think it will be worthwhile to look at service design and the management domain as overlapping areas that can contribute fluently across borders.

Notes

1 www.fimecc.com/content/uxus-user-experience-and-usability-complex-systems.
2 Credits for the design to Juha Johansson and Katrine Øverlie Svela.
3 Credits for the design to Thomas Wahl and Zhenzhen Gu.

References

Bitner, M. J., Ostrom, A. and Morgan, F. (2008) Service blueprinting: A practical technique for service innovation. *California Management Review*, Spring, pp. 66–94.
Gruber, M., de Leon, N., George, G. and Thompson, P. (2015) Managing by design. *Academy of Management Journal*, *58*(1), pp. 1–7.
Lu, Y. and Roto, V. (2015) Evoking meaningful experiences at work: A positive design framework for work tools. *Journal of Engineering Design: Special Issue on Interaction and Experience Design*, *26*(4–6), pp. 99–120.
Mattelmäki, T. and Lehtonen, K. (2006) Designing alternative arrangements for ageing workers. *Proceedings of Participatory Design Conference 2006* (pp. 101–104), Palo Alto, CA: CPSR.
Matveinen, J-V., Kronqvist J., Vaajakallio, K. and Koivisto, M. (2015) Systematic implementation of service design: A transformation framework. *Touchpoint*, *7*(1), pp. 42–45.
Saco, R.M. and Goncalves, A.P. (2008) Service design. An appraisal. *Design Management Review*. *19*(2), pp. 10–19.

3 Applications of service design in the software industry

Service design practices of understanding, mapping and collaborating through Autodesk

Pelin Arslan

Keywords: Autodesk, user-centric culture, role of service designer, user experience, workshop, co-creation

This chapter discusses how service design helps a software company become more customer-centric and interconnected. The article aims to create a practical framework to guide the service-design practices of understanding, mapping and collaborating in an organisational setting. The cases will formulate and illustrate the strategic and tactical contribution of service design in service development and delivery, showing how it drives user-centric cultural change. The analysis of the best practices reflects the opportunities of engagement models and feedback loops, outlining the need for more integrated service-design programmes.

Autodesk: transition towards a user-centric culture

Autodesk is a software company offering services to a variety of customers in the fields of architecture, engineering and construction, manufacturing and digital media and entertainment markets. Autodesk, which started as an engineering-driven company, is now moving towards a user-centric culture that integrates new technologies, cloud-based collaboration services and subscription-based business models. Cloud technologies allow people to connect different product workflows and share capabilities with teams in a centralised workspace, anywhere and anytime. In the past, the company tended to have a more policy-driven approach with a high investment in business-to-business interactions with partners. Partners offer pre-post purchase services (i.e. purchase a product, manage a subscription, support and educate regarding products) directly to end users. However, there was no direct relation and feedback mechanism for the actual users of the products.

Today, one-on-one and one-on-many user interactions have become crucial to success in service design and delivery. Entering into new markets with acquisitions in the fields of manufacturing, the future of making things and the

Internet of Things allowed the company to change its strategy from selling products to creating meaningful relationships and seamless experiences for customers. This enabled opportunities for the integration of service design to innovate and initiate user-centric service offerings.

The need for service design in an organisation

With recent transformations in technology and business, issues related to these fields are becoming more complex and demanding, as are customers' expectations. There is a great need to apply new design methods to look at the big picture and tackle new business and customer problems across connected journeys.

Service design offers toolsets that enable organisations to understand these complex problems, define better business goals and ultimately, create holistic experiences involving internal and external stakeholders. One big challenge in this domain is the application of these toolsets, and whether the company's culture is ready to accept new ways of looking at problem-solving in service innovation. Another challenge is initiating new, innovative ways of collaborating with internal stakeholders. Reviewing the literature, there is a need for service-design practices in industry settings. Recent research on mapping and developing service-design research in the UK (Sangiorgi et al. 2014), shows that there is a lack of systematic studies on how service-design agencies operate in practice, as well as how they contribute to service innovation.

Service designers connect people, processes and users. We believe that the use of a service-design approach leads to multiple perspectives that can motivate big changes in designing and executing holistic solutions, creating alignment between users' goals and company processes, and creating empathy not only towards users but also within employees, who interact with customers on a regular or daily basis as part of their jobs.

The role of a service designer in a software company

We are the only service-design team positioned in the support operations division of the company, and work closely with different teams and products to ensure customers' experience is connected, seamless and user-centred. Multidisciplinary roles are filled by the team: service designers, UX designers, content editors, programme managers and service readiness experts. The role of a service designer is to create strategic frameworks, end-to-end experience maps and compelling stories to disseminate the service-design approach throughout the organisation, by developing new methods and sharing successful outcomes.

There are certain challenges to applying service-design methods in different divisions of the company. Some divisions are not founded on design principles, and others are less likely to be open to using new methods. Design is integrated in the early stages of product development (Danish Design Center 2003), but the concept of service design does not exist. In other parts of the organisation, design is a negligible part of service development, where design decisions are based on operational metrics and business goals, but the concept of service design has different definitions. In both cases, it is important to understand the division's culture and methodology when using service design and delivery to evaluate the integration and contribution of service design.

A few tips are offered for service designers who use the service-design approach in their organisations' support operations departments:

- **Start small:** Although service design aims to look at a customer's experience holistically, as a designer it is important to start with small but strategically important projects. In particular, the business and marketing team largely owns the programmes that deliver holistic customer journeys, and design requires that incremental but impactful steps be part of these programmes.
- **Find a gap, make successful micro-pilots:** Find the gap, define the opportunity, frame the methodology and create successful small pilots to solve the problem. Successful outcomes lead to gained trust, get people talking and create interest in expanding the service-design approach to accommodate larger-scale projects.
- **Hybrid methods:** Knowledge of service-design methods is important as it helps in the creation of a strategic framework. However, it is even more crucial to find the right combination of methods and use them in the right context.
- **The outcome is more important than the methods:** Methods are necessary to tackle a problem, but do not focus only on the methods. In organisations, stakeholders are interested mostly in the outcome first, and then in the methods that were used. The trick is not to know all methods but to know how to apply them and what outcomes they lead to.
- **Show successful outcomes:** Achieving successful outcomes requires communicating success stories to stakeholders, which is crucial in organisational silos. Use outcomes to showcase how the problem was solved using service-design tools. This will aid in scaling up the project and expanding its impact.
- **Find change agents who are supportive:** Invite, inform and communicate with people who can provide support in this process. Expand your network, get their advice and use them as a sounding board to help you disseminate the work you have done using the service-design approach. These people could participate in your workshops or see your service-design methods and initiatives and, later on, utilise and benefit from them in their own work.

Service design framework

We believe that innovation results from improving our understanding of our customers and stakeholders through service-design tools. Service-design tools help teams, business owners, designers and support agents improve their ability to better serve customers and innovate. Some industry practices regarding service design include conducting user studies, establishing co-creation workshops and designing collaborative and designer-only journey maps.

We take the following three approaches for our service-design practices in the software industry: 1) understanding; 2) mapping; and 3) collaborating.

1. Understanding the user (and stakeholders)

By improving our understanding of customers' behaviour through user studies, agent interviews, case studies and community analyses, we build awareness and empathy to better design services for support operations. We use user research methods to determine customers' needs, expectations and desires for their experience, as well as to identify business opportunities and system improvements.

Gathering qualitative insights from research is extremely important to validate anecdotal assumptions from stakeholders and employees. It is important to create connections with users and include them in different stages of the design process. However, to deliver a successful user experience in an organisational setting, it is also important to include employees in the design process. Both ends contribute to using and making the experience.

New user study methods, such as user stories from an eye-tracking study that shows user participation, and collective research that shows employee engagement, promote the service-design approach in research. Visual communication of research findings and video stories are powerful tools to deliver these initiatives and increase visibility within a wider global community.

2. Mapping the experience (collaboratively)

Through journey maps and blueprints, we can walk in our customers' and company's shoes and understand what they are doing, thinking and feeling from an end-to-end holistic perspective.

We create two types of maps: designer-only and collaborative. In both processes, the input for the journey map is collected from user studies and stakeholders. However, the way in which we collect this information depends on who is creating the map. When a designer creates the journey map alone, they create the journey from a user's perspective. However, designers are not experts in the complex problems of organisations, and it is challenging to communicate and track these insights to stakeholders with control or ownership so they can be improved. For collaborative journey maps, designers frame and facilitate the mapping process, but stakeholder participation allows them to gather different perspectives and create a large, complex picture of the problem, as well as include diverse data inputs in the map. By collaborating during the creation and analysis of a journey map, participants feel more involved in the process and take responsibility for solving the problem. Collaborative journey maps hold a mirror to the organisation, reflecting different aspects and enabling us to question why we do the things we do.

We are internally developing a collaborative digital mapping tool, ATLAS (see Figure 3.1), which allows us to produce a journey map with remote team members. ATLAS is a tool for making customer journey maps that are sharable,

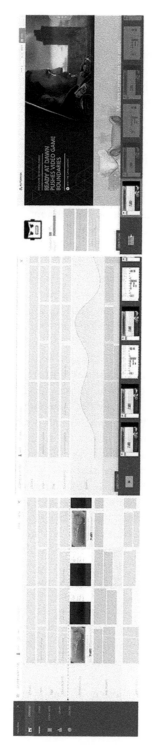

Figure 3.1 ATLAS: mapping, analysing, presenting.

informed and engaged across divisions. It allows users to map, analyse and present experience maps. The tool also allows a flexible combination of different-experience mapping techniques, from high-level end-to-end experience maps to step-by-step user journeys to blueprints. Both user and business data is integrated in the journey, which helps to prioritise the highs and lows in the customers' journey, or the most common breakdowns in backstage processes, systems and policies.

3. Collaborating with teams (and co-creating)

The success of the service depends on the alignment of teams and how they contribute to making the services as good as possible. The lack of collaboration and alignment between teams and functions results in unmet customer needs and expectations because different functions pull teams in different directions with different priorities (Reason et al. 2015). Through cross-functional journey-mapping workshops, we not only bring teams together for a shared purpose but also allow participants to focus on how they support the desired customer experience.

Based on the employee surveys we conducted after the workshops, collaborative and co-creative working sessions are excellent ways to define a roadmap, create awareness across divisions, agree on a shared point of view and gain an educational experience. We used this approach for different workshops to define a programme strategy, validate an existing design or envision the future of a service with stakeholders in the organisation.

Service design focuses on designing consistent experiences, or touchpoints, for customers. This means that service designers must not only achieve consistency and understand what people need, but also recruit the right people to develop the organisation's structure and operational effectiveness. An important component of success in designing holistic experiences is inviting team members into environments that foster a culture of collaboration, creativity and openness in which it is safe to critique.

How do service designers fit into this interdisciplinary environment? Part of our role as service designers is to ensure that people are effective individual contributors, and determine who is able to identify and nurture critical moments during the project as people look beyond their own role to see how they can contribute to the overall project. In addition, service designers must develop education that fosters skill development among employees.

Workshop approach

We have developed a workshop toolkit to guide the co-creation process. First, to define the objective, we ask business owners the following questions:

- What service, product or problem are we trying to improve, define or develop?
- How does this fit with the objectives of the organisation?
- What are we using to measure success?

These questions help us to define the objective of the workshop.

Common questions asked by the business owner are:

- How much time do you need for this journey-mapping session?
- What materials and how many participants do you need?
- Do you need any pre-work, additional preparations or resources?

These questions help business owners evaluate how much they should invest in the collaborative session, assess their resources and determine participants' time and commitment.

Once we agree to make the partnership with clear goals, we identify which end-to-end experiences we should focus on and select important scenarios, prioritising the high-level flows.

Next, we define the top three stakeholders that we should work with to achieve the goals of our workshop. Business owners suggest people that will contribute and be part of the extended core team. For generating ideas, the more the merrier, but for workshops it is ideal to work with 3–4 groups of 4–5 people with different roles. Each team involves a designer, support agent,

Figure 3.2 Workshop approach.

business owner, technical expert, content editor and, occasionally, a finance analyst, policymaker or member of top management.

There are a few challenges with co-creation workshops. One challenge is that pre-existing dynamics may exist among stakeholders, which need to be managed in the early stages of the workshop to ensure that the focus is on the workshop goals. Another challenge is that most participants are involved in many other projects, which means their attention may be diverted. Finally, it is important to understand the expected outcome and what needs to be achieved by the end of the workshop.

During the workshop, it is important to give clear instructions and examples for how participants should perform and collaborate during the mapping process. It is not easy to break down their points of view for objective contributions, but by participating they should feel more immersed in the problem and empathise with customers.

Organisations are good at starting pilots, but not always as good at taking action and leveraging what is learned. To capture the customer-centric suggestions and solution sets obtained from the workshop, we make a pool of recommendations and task business owners, who serve as group leaders in the workshop, with taking actionable steps to integrate these recommendations into their businesses. It is important to know how business owners integrate these recommendations into their strategic roadmaps in the short term, and into their programme goals in the long term. Next, the impact of these actionable items, or how many of them return the investment, is measured.

For complex programmes, a series of workshops may be best. With one workshop, your team will have a single action list, but with many workshops, an ongoing action list is created and can grow and be revised.

Conclusion

In industrial service design, we must question the ways we use the service-design framework to create additional value in businesses. There are challenges concerning the application of the service-design approach in large-scale programmes, which affects organisational goals. If your tools are not integrated into the programme or if there is not a clear engagement model, then it is difficult to track the impact of service design and measure its success over time. It is important to create tools to track and measure the impact of service design work and make sure that it is integrated into strategic roadmaps or existing implementation cycles.

Service design can help us provide sustainable value propositions and implementations for our users' ecosystems by integrating feedback loops and engagement models from three value streams into decision-making processes, and defining success with meaningful metrics. The three value streams are:

- Fostering a deep understanding of users' challenges and motivations throughout research and validation.

- Working cross-functionally with stakeholders to ensure holistic solutions.
- Partnering with thought leaders to revise customer and company goals over time.

By integrating these feedback loops using service-design tools, we become user-centric advocates, trusted advisers, valuable collaborators and visionary leaders in the design ecosystem of an organisation.

Service design provides customer-focus alignment and employee participation, and deals with internal challenges concerning systems, processes and policies. It is crucial to create new engagement models with internal and external stakeholders to understand the impact of service design in an organisational setting. The best engagement does not just inform and require change, but also solicits insights, ideas and feedback from employees to ensure that the changes are optimised. Employees should feel included and be aware of the decisions made with thought leaders.

In this engagement model, research and strategy must be translated into action and impact. A step-by-step framework in the form of a workbook to translate user needs and business goals into purposeful programmatic solutions could deliver high-quality outcomes for and from our users, while bringing value to the company. This framework could then be used to create new user-centric programmes and improve existing ones to endure end-to-end customer experiences. Journey maps across products, users and business models could be supported by concrete actions, resource requirements and business and user validation. These elements could build towards the strategy that you will craft to accomplish your service-design goals.

To conclude, it is important to use service-design tools (user studies, journey maps and blueprints) to drive strategic initiatives and user-centric programmes to sustain the use of a service-design approach for feedback loops and engagement models within a company. Service design needs to be fully integrated into large-scale programmes to drive change in the organisation. It is crucial that these kinds of journey-mapping workshops are accepted as a framework and are integrated into the structure of a programme for creating a value stream to be embedded into strategic planning. To ensure a more sustainable approach for our feedback loops, these methods need to be fully integrated into cross-divisional programmes.

We need more examples of service design in various industry settings. Since service design is a reflective practice in which service designers can reflect on actions taken in order to improve the service-design methodology, we can continuously develop our methods and frameworks.

References

Danish Design Center (2003) Design Ladder, the 4 Levels of Design Maturity, the Economic Effects of Design. Retrieved from www.seeplatform.eu/casestudies/Design%20Ladder (accessed 29 February, 2016).

Reason, B., Lovlie, L. and Brand Flu, M. (2015) *Service Design for Business: A Practical Guide to Optimizing the Customer Experience*. Hoboken, NJ: John Wiley.

Sangiorgi, D., Prendiville, A. and Ricketts, A. (2014) Mapping and Developing Service Design Research in the UK. Project Report. Lancaster, UK: AHRC.

4 Materialising contexts through design for service narratives

Katarina Wetter Edman

Keywords: context through narratives technique, value co-creation, materialisation, resource integration

Service, service innovation and service design have experienced several modes of development. When services are seen as a market segment in relation to products, certain characteristics of the services become important, such as their immateriality, heterogeneity, inseparability from the product, perishability (IHIP), and the fact that they are created at the moment of consumption. These are often referred to as the IHIP characteristics. Service can also be seen as the value that is created when things, people and systems interact, and the relations, experiences, knowledge and contexts involved in these value-creation situations become important, also known as service (dominant) logic (Vargo and Lusch 2004). Service design as a design practice first evolved as a complement to product design, addressing the specificities of services; however, it has increasingly taken on a service-logic position and is conceptualised as an approach to service innovation and designing for service. This is fruitful since a service-logic perspective brings attention to the importance of understanding aspects of value co-creation that lie in the core of design practice, such as experience, context and participation (Meroni and Sangiorgi 2011; Wetter Edman et al. 2014).

When service is viewed as value co-creation, the distinction between goods (products) and service becomes blurred. Goods are seen as mediators of service, so instead of focusing on the development of specific goods, designers consider the context in which goods are used, how they are used and prior experience and knowledge of the people involved with the goods. Thus, the complexity increases and the properties of the physical goods become one of several aspects that need to be considered. In short, value-in-use and value-in-context are at the core of what needs to be understood for making service innovation happen. Although service logic states that value is always uniquely and phenomenologically determined by the beneficiary, Grönroos and Voima (2013) position the customer as an actor who both creates and evaluates value over time in an experiential process of usage. They argue:

> Therefore, in the same way that the firm controls the production process and can invite the customer to join it as a co-producer of resources (e.g. Eiglier and

Langeard 1975), the customer controls the experiential value creation process and may invite the service provider to join this process as a co-creator of value.

(Grönroos and Voima 2013: 138)

Based on this argument, the authors further suggest that service providers should consider how they could be involved in customers' lives rather than expecting customers to be involved with the service providers. For this purpose, they proposed three spheres that could help position the locus of value creation: the provider sphere, the customer sphere and the joint sphere. Value co-creation can only occur in the joint sphere, and value creation can only occur in the customer sphere. To some extent, this opposes the idea of value as always being co-created; in the provider sphere, value can only be facilitated (Grönroos and Voima 2013).

This perspective relates directly to what is often considered to be the last step in the process of servitisation: starting with the service supporting the product, followed by the services supporting product usage and, finally, the services supporting customers' processes (Oliva and Kallenberg 2003). Profound knowledge about customers' processes and an understanding of which service provider actions are perceived as valuable are necessary to achieve servitisation. The challenge is to make these material and social practices tangible and usable for service innovation purposes.

This chapter explores how service designers materialise use-narratives, or stories about material and social practices, to make contexts and user experiences urgent and relevant for industrial service organisations to act upon.

Design practices, narratives and design materials

Design for service emphasises participatory methods; since services are co-created, it is necessary to involve the different stakeholders in the development process. Implications for design practice include an increased focus on how to manage and set up collaborative events. This in turn affects the role and perception of what designers contribute in collaborative design settings. Instead of being competent individuals that control the outcome, the designer leads and facilitates the activities and produces material artefacts, thereby establishing a situation in which interactions take place.

Materialised talk as design material

Service design is a design practice where material aspects are often downplayed. Instead, relational aspects are highlighted, although how they are represented throughout design work is not evident. Drawing on Schön and his theories of reflective practice, Eriksen (2012) argues that talk can be material in (co-)design situations. She further explores and defines practices connected to materialisation in co-design by identifying five moves. First:

with a focus on the move from *materials* – through *materializing* – to *materialized*; second, with a focus on how negotiating of meaning of *content materials* is an integral part of *materializing* in co-designing; third, with a focus on how delegation of roles to materials largely is a part of the organizer's planned *formatting* of an event; fourth, with a focus on how tangible *formats* and *content materials* merge in the process of *materializing* during a co-design situation; and lastly, how the invitation and introduction of new *formats* during an event can assist in a transformative process of *materializing*.

(Eriksen 2012: 245; italics in original)

Talk and stories are increasingly used as design material in the design for service approach (Grimaldi et al. 2013). Narratives function as a bridge between the sphere of customers and the sphere of the organisation (Cayla and Arnould 2013), or as mediators among different actors, their situations and the potential future, relying on a narrative's potential to hold and organise meaning and experiences and to embody both complexity and simplicity (Bruner 1991). Narratives are considered to capture the complexities of service, including the cultural and social aspects of events for service innovation purposes, as well as the particularities of each situation (Viña and Mattelmäki 2010).

Empirical illustration

The following illustration draws on an ethnographic study of design collaboration with an industrial dairy equipment manufacturer, IndComp. The author and a colleague conducted a micro-level empirical analysis of a user-involvement workshop. The workshop was led by a design firm as part of a service design pilot, in order to gain a deeper understanding of what the customers – dairy farmers with an automatic milking machine – experienced as value-creating situations. The introduction of such highly automated equipment in farmers' lives changes the situations in which value co-creation takes place, as well as which resources are available for them to integrate.

The workshop used the context through narratives (CTN) technique (Wetter Edman and Magnusson 2016), focusing on how stories of experiences are captured and then developed into design narratives, specifically from the information that designers obtained from users' stories. A collaborative set-up for the design dialogue encouraged farmers to tell stories about positive and negative experiences in relation to six predefined situations. These stories were written down, and descriptive photos were added to create a document referred to as an 'instantiation' (see Figure 4.1). Afterwards, the participants jointly constructed a landscape of the matter of concern.

The instantiations, as the physical outputs from the workshop, were the focus of the analysis. The instantiations can be seen as the designers' direct interpretation and materialisation of the farmers' accounts, or the result of negotiations between the farmers and designers in the workshop setting. A total of 28 instantiations and 113 sticky notes were collected as physical outputs from the workshop, including an additional situation/theme with a single instantiation that emerged during the workshop. Thematic analysis based on coding and construction of themes was performed (Braun and Clarke 2006).

Figure 4.1 Illustration from workshop with designers and farmers.

Since the instantiations included short sentences and/or keywords, the readings were supported by transcriptions of audio recordings from the workshop to improve participants' understanding of the readings. Figure 4.2 shows an example of an instantiation and how it was related to the transcription.

Situation: Before Service	Title: Flexibility	Evaluation: Good
Description in text on instantiations (B2):	The service technician adapts to the situation at the farm (within a time span of ex 2 weeks) (can be "too flexible") – may sometimes give an impression of being strained	
Transcription:	(0:04:08.1) Farmer 1: The service technician adapts his schedule, so he is flexible in regards to the one that runs the farm if it is harvest etc. (0:04:38.7) This can also be a negative thing, this, because sometimes the service technician can be too flexible, I think at least. It can be too long intervals [between service]. (0:04:47.9) Facilitator Richard: you feel that... (0:04:50.2) [Designer1, Victor writes something on sticky note] Farmer 1: I feel that the problems increase if it takes longer Facilitator Richard: Hmm... So the problems increase... Farmer 1: it may yes... function less well right before service. They seem at times very strained, the service technicians it is easy to push the service forward, they have a lot of extra [work], and this is not so good. ... But that he reschedules it when I want it that is another thing. [Laughter]

Figure 4.2 Example of instantiation.

The findings

The analysis indicated that materialisation enabled the designers to pay specific attention to the following three themes: 1) service characteristics and socio-technical contexts; 2) resources from the farmers' perspective; and 3) dependencies and tensions. The themes and the categories are described below in relation to the analysed data.

Service characteristics and socio-technical context

As expected, the designers paid attention to the relations, activities and interactions comprising the service offering. Remarkably, only one-third of the instantiations said something exclusively about the producer or user sphere. Two-thirds of the instantiations accounted for the relation between these two spheres, thus situating the materialisations in the joint value-creation sphere. This drew attention to the situations and contexts in which the farmer acted.

The textbook design literature argues for the importance of understanding the users' context and what constitutes it without providing further details. Context is defined as what surrounds and affects the interaction with the product/technology. Additional analysis of our data showed that a majority of the instantiations mentioned technology or interactions with technology – the automatic milking machine (AMM) equipment – briefly or not at all, focusing instead on the farmers' experiences and perspectives. In these descriptions, the farmers' processes and practices were given priority. For example, to identify the pace of work, the designers did not inquire about the AMM per se but asked the farmers: How is work at the farm overall? One instantiation captured the altered pace of work when attention needed to be paid to the robot instead of to the cows' need to be milked. In effect, this demanded a complete transformation of how the farmer organised the daily work around the AMM. Although the work was still organised around the activity of milking, it was not the cows that set the pace, but rather the machinery. The social aspects of what it was like to be a farmer with an AMM then became visible.

The materialised stories emphasise that it is not what the farmers or service technicians do with technology that is the focus, but what the technology does within the farmers' context. The instantiations focus on relations between the user and technology and how these relations affect the farmers' everyday lives. This extends the scope of the service characteristics to include the farmers' socio-technical context.

Resource integration from the farmers' perspective

The initial situations in the workshop consistently asked about previous experiences and memories. They either focused explicitly on the users' own experiences or asked if they could retell specific good or poor events. That is, the farmers were asked to talk about things they knew and experienced and reflect on the existing relationship they had with the company.

One instantiation materialised in a discussion about a specific service situation of the AMM, when the cows needed to be milked before or during the service time. This put extra pressure on the farmers to prepare before the service period, so when service was cancelled at short notice, unnecessary work had been carried out. Through this materialisation, the designers brought attention to the fact that small changes in routines could make large differences in convenience for the farmers. In the example, the service technician received an emergency call during the night and had to cancel the upcoming planned service. According to the story, this was done at very short notice. However, the solution was provided within the story: a text message could be sent to the farmer when the planned service was cancelled. Several of the instantiations displayed how the behaviour of the service technician – being friendly, stressed, tired and so on – strongly influenced farmers' experience of the service.

The materialisations represent resources from a user perspective, which is to be expected. However, what is highlighted is how the resources are used and what this means in relation to the farmer's own organisation. Thus, the materialisations show how both the farmers' and the organisations' resources and practices are important.

Dependencies and tensions

The co-creative nature of service implies that resources from both the provider and customer spheres are integrated into service delivery. In both the themes described above, the tensions and dependencies between the farmer and company materialised and were exposed in the instantiations. For example, the AMM needed to be cleaned before service, but who did this was not stated. The farmer expected the service technician to do it, and vice versa. Similar to the previous example of how preparatory milking was conducted, successful and less successful integrations of resources were presented. Here, the farmer prepared the equipment and production units – the cows – for service, which was carried out by the service technician. The farmer used his organisational resources to help the service organisation do its job and supposedly to minimise costs and ensure mutual benefits, which can be seen as co-creation. However, the captured narratives showed that this co-creation was not unproblematic.

If any of the partners do not do what is expected of them, there are implications for the other party. This is called *conditional integration*, meaning that one of the partners is affected by the other partner's actions, although the outcome depends on the integration of their resources. Understanding how the farmers moved and interacted with the protocols brings focus to the contextual aspects of service. How this integration is carried out and possibly altered is an area open to interpretation and thus potential innovation.

Discussion

This study used a detailed analysis of instantiations made by designers and the farmers' accounts of their previous experiences, to explore what the designers paid attention to in the materialisation of the users' accounts in the workshop, and how this was relevant for the industrial organisation.

Materialising service characteristics and socio-technical contexts

The researchers expected that what the designers materialised would focus on the service characteristics, since these are aspects that are used to improve service design. They also expected that the workshop would provide information about the users and their context since the designer selected the method and developed it for this purpose. However, it was surprising that the focus on the socio-technical context was so prominent and that the actual products were quite marginal. The use of the product was not the focus; instead, attention was focused on the effect the product/system and interactions with the service-providing organisation had on the customer's life, which extends the dominant conceptualisation of context to include anything that surrounds the use of a product.

In research on experience-centric services, context has been defined as consisting of the physical and relational elements in the experience environment, including the physical setting, social actors and social interactions with other customers and/or service facilitators (Zomerdijk and Voss 2010). This study shows that these contextual aspects are important even in industrial services.

Furthermore, the materialisations of the users' accounts can be seen as a way to operationalise this understanding of context. Context is often understood as a somewhat blurry description of almost everything and everyone that is involved before, during and after a specific service encounter. By exemplifying the farmers' practices in the instantiations, the designers made the context explicit and possible to work with for future solutions.

In addition, the attention paid to resources and how they are integrated suggests that the designers were focused implicitly on value co-creation. The designers' materialisations of resources and their interactions resulted in a shift from a traditional understanding of services as products to an expanded understanding of service as value creation.

Materialising tensions and opportunities

Materialisations document what specific activities and interactions mean in and for customers' everyday and professional lives. This is often done through a display of tensions between the user and the company's organisations. Something perceived as positive from one perspective necessarily has implications for the other. Several of the instantiations include these dual perspectives, which exposes an opportunity for further development. This finding mirrors Kimbell's thoughts on the tensions in service design: 'On the one hand, service designers pay attention to the artefacts that are part of services, but on the other, they are concerned with how the relations between people and artifacts create value or result in change' (Kimbell 2013: 15). The analysis also suggests that the designers use an implicit practice perspective by focusing on the users' practices, showing how the industrial organisation affects them by inhibiting some and promoting others.

Conclusion

In this example of farmers' experiences with AMMs, the narratives focus on the users' context and practice rather than individual products or services. The instantiations are used to materialise the entangled experiences of use, context and practice, and to propose new practices that are beneficial for both the customer and the industrial company.

Context is treated as a fairly abstract concept in the service-logic literature. This study shows how context can be made concrete by constructing stories of both existing and future contexts. The designers use the integrated information from both the user and the company to propose new service opportunities. In doing so, the designers show the company the importance of understanding what their activities mean and how they impact the users' organisations.

The designers in this study not only attend to the practices but also explicitly use the farmers' experiences as a starting point, by questioning previous specific service experiences and interactions between the farmer and the firm. Moreover, they open the scope of inquiry to include the farmers' lives in general, and thus reach out into a context that is outside the firm, or, as it is termed by Grönroos and Voima (2013), the 'customer sphere'.

Note

This study was carried out with funding from the Torsten Söderberg Foundation, Project E44/10, Making Sense of Design Work.

References

Braun, V. and Clarke, V. (2006) Using thematic analysis in psychology. *Qualitative Research in Psychology, 3*(2), pp. 77–101.

Bruner, J.S. (1991) The narrative construction of reality. *Critical Inquiry, 18*(1), pp. 1–21.

Cayla, J. and Arnould, E. (2013) Ethnographic stories for market learning. *Journal of Marketing, 77*(4), pp. 1–16.

Eiglier, P. and Langeard, E. (1975) *Une Approche nouvelle du marketing des services, Revue Francaise de Gestion, 2* (November).

Eriksen, M.A. (2012) Material matters in co-designing: Formatting and staging with participating materials in co-design projects, events and situations (dissertation). Malmö: Faculty of Culture and Society, Malmö University.

Grimaldi, S., Fokkinga, S. and Ocnarescu, I. (2013) Narratives in design: A study of the types, applications and functions of narratives in design practice. *Proceedings of the 6th International Conference on Designing Pleasurable Products and Interfaces* (pp. 201–210). New York: ACM.

Grönroos, C. and Voima, P. (2013) Critical service logic: Making sense of value creation and co-creation. *Journal of the Academy of Marketing Science, 41*(2), pp. 133–150. DOI 10.1007/s11747-012-0308-3.

Kimbell, L. (2013) An inventive practice perspective on designing (doctoral dissertation). Lancaster, UK: Lancaster University.

Meroni, A. and Sangiorgi, D. (2011) *Design for Services*, Surrey: Gower.

Oliva, R. and Kallenberg, R. (2003) Managing the transition from products to services. *International Journal of Service Industry Management, 14*(2), pp. 160–172.

Vargo, S.L. and Lusch, R.F. (2004) Evolving to a new dominant logic of marketing. *Journal of Marketing, 68*(1), pp. 1–17.

Viña, S. and Mattelmäki, T. (2010) Spicing up public journeys: Storytelling as a design strategy. In: *ServDes, 2nd Nordic Conference on Service Design and Service Innovation*, 1–3 December, 2010 (pp. 77–86). Linköping: Linköping University Electronic Press.

Wetter Edman, K. and Magnusson, P.R. (2016) Capturing context through service design stories. In: M.G. Luchs, K.S. Swan and A. Griffin (Eds.), *Design Thinking: New Product Development Essentials from the PDMA* (pp. 237–252). Hoboken, NJ: John Wiley.

Wetter Edman, K., Sangiorgi, D., Edvardsson, B., Holmlid, S., Grönroos, C. and Mattelmäki, T. (2014) Design for value co-creation: Exploring the synergies between design for service and service logic. *Service Science, 6*(2), pp. 106–121.

Zomerdijk, L.G. and Voss, C.A. (2010) Service design for experience-centric services. *Journal of Service Research, 13*(1), pp.67– 82. DOI: 10.1177/1094670509351960.

5 Service design at scale

Bernadette Geuy

Keywords: University of California, Berkeley, Student Information System (SIS) Project, outside in, inside out, scale up, customer journey, user experience

Large-scale and industrial-sized changes provide a rare opportunity for an organisation to significantly transform its business operations through service design; to look holistically and cross-functionally at how end users (students, faculty and staff in this higher education case study) navigate core business services; and to re-imagine service experiences that are user-centred and journey-based. The larger the scale of the business change, the greater the potential to radically transform business processes and improve end-user experiences, which are the key drivers of the University of California, Berkeley's investment in its Student Information Systems (SIS) project.

This case study describes the service design approach employed by the Project's User Experience (UX) Portal team: designing at scale and working outside in and inside out to transform service delivery, with the overarching goal of supporting students' success through their academic careers.

UC Berkeley's Student Information Systems (SIS) project

The University of California (UC), Berkeley, was founded in 1868. It is the pre-eminent public research university in the world, with a student body of over 37,000 and a world-renowned faculty that includes seven Nobel Laureates. In 2014, UC Berkeley made a strategic decision to replace its constellation of ageing, disparate and internally built and maintained student systems with a modern, nimble and effective vendor-supported system that includes admissions, enrolment, registration, financial aid, student accounts and advising. This new system is accessed via a UC Berkeley-developed portal called CalCentral, which smooths the inclusion of a multitude of experiences while providing visual consistency and a voice to the Berkeley brand.

A project this large and ambitious cannot be successful without some key ingredients, including strong leadership and a high-calibre, dedicated team that is united around a common purpose to transform student business service delivery on campus. The initiative must be well scoped and adequately funded to cover the required project costs and ongoing operations budget. Additionally, sponsors, stakeholders and end users play a critical role in driving the case for change, as well as providing ongoing input, governance oversight and change management support.

UC Berkeley's students have been very active in calls for large-scale changes to the online student systems. Student groups on campus, including the student government, participated in the Requests for Proposal (RFP) requirements phase, as well as workshops and user research, and as team members, the students performed UX design, communications, development, quality assurance (QA) and training support.

Defining and anchoring design work around core university journeys

When dissecting the core workings of a university and its primary role in higher education, class offerings and the activities of teaching, learning and research are central to the institution. Administrative and planning activities that support academic programmes, curriculum development, as well as planning and enrolment for students come next. Advising, financial aid and billing, and all the underlying administrative functions and student record-keeping, support these core functions. The entrance and exit points on this model are admissions and graduation, respectively.

Students, faculty and staff traverse these university education functions on *journeys*. For the SIS project, we identified five *archetype* journeys that represent the paths, goals and drivers of end users across one or more of these core functions (Liedtka et al. 2014). These archetypal journeys helped the UX team orient themselves for macro-level service design, and in considering the placement of digital touchpoints on CalCentral, the University's portal.

The identified journeys are representative of the context and scope of the SIS project, which is replacing the admissions, student records, financial aid, student billing, class enrolment and advice systems.

Designing outside in and inside out

As a service designer, the primary objective is to understand the journeys and goals of end users and to design from a user-centred, or outside-in, perspective (Manning and Bodine 2012). The different *touchpoints*, digital and non-digital interactions related to each journey, must be identified to design for the most seamless, intuitive and goal-supporting set of experiences. For industrial service design, and when designing at scale, the impacted business units and service providers play a crucial role in the service design model. Design work at this scale must encompass and support delivery of the functional business processes, and necessitates incorporating a strong inside-out perspective. Thus, the role of the service designer is to learn, interpret, navigate and design the best possible service experiences that honour the needs of end users, as well as the business units that serve them – to work outside in and inside out.

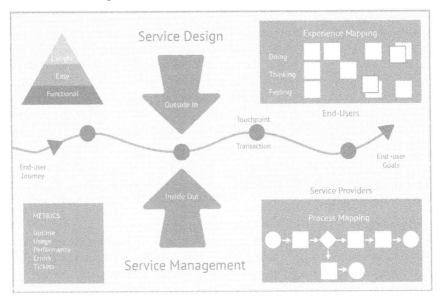

Figure 5.1 Designing the experience: outside in and inside out.

Outside in: journey-mapping the 'as-is' and other research methods

Journey and experience mapping have been core methods by which the needs and desires of end users have been collected and used to drive UC Berkeley's service design work. The UX team has developed design briefs and maps for the core journeys identified, and they provide an invaluable view of the as-is pathways, end-user motivations and the opportunity areas for service improvements.

To ensure a strong outside-in point of view, students have been engaged in numerous ways. Over twenty UC Berkeley students have been hired as team members for the project. Other students have participated in design studios, and been surveyed and challenged through an innovation-focused student group to conduct user research and design studio parts. Additionally, the project team is working closely with student government to support outreach, communications and change management plans.

Near the beginning of the project, and before any new functionality had been delivered, a usability and learnability survey was conducted to benchmark how students view the legacy systems experience. Students were randomly asked to provide their feedback on different aspects of the online experience, including billing and payments, financial aid, academic planning and enrolment. The results and low scores confirmed the need for change and provided a valuable baseline for demonstrating quantitatively the impact of the SIS project and service improvements over time.

Additionally, one-on-one interviews, the development of student personas and ad-hoc user testing were used by the UX team to collect input, and to verify how end users relate to preliminary designs. These, along with the output of other research techniques, helped the team make the case for design decisions when working with our functional business partners.

Inside out: translating self-service specifications to journeys and touchpoints

For the SIS project, the UX design team spends a high proportion of its time interacting with the functional business team members in agile sprints. As noted previously, the functional teams have a need to assess and replace their current business processes, update the underlying technology and deliver new services to the end users. What are commonly defined by the project as *self-service* items are digital *touchpoints*, where personalised information is presented to an end user, and where a transaction or workflow can be initiated. The functional teams develop functional specifications that describe their *self-service* items, the underlying data structures and states, business rules and so on, and these become the input and starting point for service design sprints.

It is worth noting that *outside-in* and *inside-out* perspectives do not align very well (Gray and Vander Wal 2014), as a business process with transactions does not equate well to a journey with cross-functional *touchpoints*. End users navigate service offerings *horizontally* across touchpoints and across service providers. Service providers and functional business teams, on the other hand, look inside out and *vertically* at where end users interact with their particular business unit. An example of this is *Academic Planning and Enrolment*, which involves two functional teams. Each of these teams is responsible for different online tools, such as the schedule of classes and the enrolment 'shopping cart', which are managed by Student Records, and the four-year planner, appointment notes and progress report, which are maintained by Advising. To a student, however, these are simply academic planning tools.

Optimally, the UX design team clusters related work into sprints so that the self-service requests map to an end-user experience or a related set of experiences. In the case of Academic Planning and Enrolment, the designer must provide students with a way to navigate between the various tools with ease as they review their plans for the upcoming term. Students need to look at classes they must still take to meet their major requirements, see what is being offered this term to fulfil a requirement, explore topics and other classes of interest, and fit all their desired classes into their schedule prior to submitting their enrolment request. This workflow will involve interacting with five to six tools, and the goal is to make the flow as intuitive and seamless as possible.

Designing and synthesising the 'to be' user experiences

Traditionally, work on a large industrial-scale project is organised and oriented from the perspective of the business units, inside out and prioritised by the business process to meet the project's various delivery deadlines. Service designers must therefore create a draft project model of how and where different self-service items will be presented in the portal at the end of the project. This helps to maintain a macro outside-in focus and to ensure the delivery of impactful and supportive journey-based vs. transactional experiences. For UC Berkeley, the UX team mapped out a *Card Board*, initially with Post-It notes and then digitally, of the end-of-project state of CalCentral, with all its pages and requisite cards on each. During the design sprints, assumptions about which cards would be needed to include the new functionality and experiences were validated and refined, and then the *Card Board* was updated.

As service designers, the team members must be able to make the requisite service experience connections between their user research and their work with functional owners and technical specifications. By design, it is the designer's job to weave self-service transaction needs into touchpoints and the larger journey view.

What the portal team is able to provide is the ability to see how all of these functional areas dovetail into a unified experience that is relatively seamless to the student. Good service design takes a set of self-service items – in the case of the SIS project – and melds them into a union that is stronger than the individual components on their own. This creates the possibility for transforming a once cumbersome workflow into something that enhances the journey, and supports the end user in successfully reaching their academic goals. Beyond having strong user-experience research and design skills, the portal team members must be strategic systems thinkers who understand the functional interplay and are able to translate, design for and navigate the project's complex business, technical and user-experience needs.

Large-scale design constraints and opportunities

Designing at scale will certainly be constrained within the context of a large project, where time and resources limit the level of design work that can be accomplished, as well as the degree to which transformational service improvements can be achieved. Without extensive time to research and perform user testing, smaller details of the design will not receive the attention they deserve (i.e. micro-copy finessing and validating design choices with end users).

While the service designer is armed with knowledge of many needs from the research, it is nearly impossible to synthesise all the features and opportunities into the initial releases. As an experienced UX team has learned, it is often best to implement a viable design and learn from end users what the follow-on opportunities are, as delivering something transformational may not yet be possible given the current understanding of the needs and capabilities of the underlying technology. Additionally, a project plan cannot fully anticipate nor include all the possible service improvements that could be delivered. By its nature, a large project is oriented primarily around delivering a working set of systems along with the requisite workflows and transactions, such that operations are not interrupted or degraded by the complex changes that are being made.

With this in mind, UX designers and their functional business partners will make service choices. At a minimum, the design will ensure that all transactions (touchpoints) are in place and accessible through a well-thought-out information architecture, and that the end user can find the self-service items they are looking for with reasonable ease. A more desirable outcome is that end-users' information and transaction needs are met clearly, in context and prescriptively, that is, that decision-making options are clearly presented along with relevant and well-presented supporting data, and that the end-user's path to this point, as well as their next steps (the journey), are incorporated into the design. Ultimately, and with the right portal platform, the designs can be increasingly proactive, alerting and guiding the end user in decision-making by suggesting appropriate courses of action.

Design agilely within a waterfall-type project plan

Because the UX/Portal team is relatively small, it is impossible to track the activities of five functional teams for the duration of the project. Instead, the team has employed three-week agile sprints to do a deep dive on a particular functional team's set of *self-service* offerings (i.e. to review and understand the specifications then conduct the requisite research, business analysis and design work).

The SIS project is being managed through a waterfall-type project plan with seven predefined functional release dates over the course of nine months. Within this project, the UX team is tracking three-week design sprints based on priority and release-date sequence. This constrained window of time focuses both the design team and the functional team members on business functions that must be delivered through self-service, while the UX team looks at the service flows and related journey maps to maximise the impact of the new service experiences. Both teams start the sprint with a planning and scope meeting and identify research needs. Throughout the sprint, there are daily Stand Up meetings and ad-hoc design meetings to gain clarity on the specifications or a business rule, for example, or to map out the workflow. A minimum of two Functional Design Acceptance meetings are held to secure approvals on card designs before they are assigned to the Portal and Application Program Interface (API) development teams.

Transforming experiences with UC Berkeley's CalCentral[1] portal

A key strategic decision was to leverage the Berkeley-developed portal, *CalCentral*, as the primary online services delivery platform for campus community members. Launched in January 2014, CalCentral has incrementally been delivering a unified face to UC Berkeley's many academic, administrative and financial services. CalCentral is a lightweight integration platform that was developed by staff using Ruby on Rails and Angular JS to expose, repackage and present the users' personal data, sourced from a number of legacy systems, with the aim of *unifying, simplifying, informing, alerting* and *supporting students' success.* The responsive design works equally well on mobile and traditional desktop platforms. The platform abstracts the end user and their data from the underlying systems through the use of APIs. The design of user experience is centred around service design disciplines that are user journey vs. functional business units based (outside → in).

Unlike a traditional portal that may be purchased with a vendor's student information system, with functionality limited to curated links and *portlets* (windows into the underlying system), CalCentral is a highly flexible and lightweight platform, where each screen has been designed from the end-user's perspective. The *My Finances* page of CalCentral, for example, includes a snapshot of the student's bill, their financial aid summary (budget and awards), the balance on their campus meal points and debit card, as well as a number of financial resources. Behind this page are secondary pages that detail the student's financial transactions and lead them through a rich set of financial aid actions, such as accepting a loan or comparing aid packages. Student Billing and Financial Aid data are sourced by business functions in two different departments, but to a student they are all part of *My Finances*.

Case study: advising, academic planning and service design in support of students' success

The roles and service journeys of advising staff and students intersect over academic planning. Together, they share a strong interest in the student's academic success as well as their physical, emotional and financial well-being. The interplay at touchpoints, shared by advising staff and students' journeys, are transformational service design opportunities, and these junctions are where the UX team has the greatest opportunity to contribute to contextual understanding, information transparency, decision-making and ultimately to students' success.

Well-designed planning tools, along with timely information, support students and their advisers as they navigate the complexities of completing a rigorous university academic programme. An important shared tool that has

Figure 5.2 Academic planning: student and adviser journeys.

been added through the SIS project is an academic planner, which the adviser can populate with a prescribed set of classes to meet the needs of the university, as well as the student's chosen major. Together, an adviser and their student will discuss academic interests prior to declaring a major, and the planner will become their shared understanding of how the student can meet graduation requirements within the time and unit constraints of the university. Each year, the plan can be revised and adjusted as classes are completed and as the student's academic goals and major selection solidify.

Design input to support these advising touchpoints included a design studio workshop for students, where participants explored their as-is process for planning and selecting classes in which to enrol. The students also identified the strong need to unify access to the many tools and steps that they take, leading up to and following their scheduled class enrolment dates. Overall, students want to know: How am I doing? Will I graduate on time? There was also an overarching desire by students to reduce uncertainty in their plans, to know whether they would get a seat in one or more desirable classes, and to have a reasonable degree of confidence in their ability to perform successfully in the upcoming term.

For advisers, the UX team interviewed a number of staff members, with a particular interest in how they manage a large student caseload, their typical daily activities and what they need to support their advising appointments. Advisers are skilled at guiding academic progress, as well as scanning student records to spot problems and to perform interventions. We had the opportunity to codify data that is well understood by seasoned advising staff and to create an easy-to-read set of student success criteria and milestone data. To design an adviser's dashboard, it was important for us to know what elements of a student's record the advisers review on a regular basis, how they assess this data, what actions they take and under what conditions they take those actions.

The resulting service design for advising and academic planning is an Adviser Dashboard for caseload management and to support individual advising appointments. Easy access to the planner, academic progress report, appointment notes, student success and milestones indicators and enrolment history are included. For students, their My Academics dashboard includes academic planning and enrolment tools, including the academic planner, academic progress reports, action items and notes from the adviser, success and milestone indicators, enrolment dates and a transcript of completed classes. Shared planning information and access to progress and success indicators support better decision-making, increase self-service access and help to make advising appointments richer and more holistic.

Conclusion

In conclusion, service design at scale, working both outside in and inside out in agile sprints, has proven to be an effective way to capture and design for the journeys and needs of our end users while fulfilling the self-service delivery requirements of our functional business owners. All this is done to achieve the goals of transforming service delivery and supporting students' success, as illustrated in the advising and academic planning example on page 50 (Figure 5.2).

Note

1 www.calcentral.berkeley.edu.

References

Gray, D. and Vander Wal, T. (2014) *The Connected Company*. Sebastopol, CA: O'Reilly Media.

Liedtka, J., Ogilvie, T. and Brozenske, R. (2014) *The Designing for Growth Field Book*. New York: Columbia Business School.

Manning, H. and Bodine, K. (2012) *Outside In: The Power of Putting your Customers at the Center of your Business*. Las Vegas: Amazon.

6 Industrial service design in China

Bo Gao and Gabriele Tempesta

Keywords: One foundation, branding, urbanisation, China, service quality, customer experience, sustainability

After decades of rapid economic growth in China, intensive industry transition and social problems have arisen. In recent years, industrial service design has begun to play an increasingly significant role in industry transformation, helping to improve service efficiency, customer experience and improving corporate image.

With the recent global financial crisis, the new wave of information technology has driven industrial and commercial changes deeper, and impacted fundamentally the traditional business environment. China has gradually accumulated advantages in both hardware and software development, owing to its vast manufacturing base. The latest 'Internet+' strategy (Keqiang 2015) integrates mobile Internet, cloud computing and Big Data. Social–network platforms have created new media centres for corporations and individuals to communicate and share their ideas. Industrial service design has the opportunity to implement the Internet+ strategy and stand out with competitive advantages.

Urbanisation in China has been one of the crucial aspects of China's contemporary development process. The imbalance of population distribution and the severe ageing of the population have already put pressure on the country's resources, public service capabilities and sustainable development. China's Government has been betting on urbanisation as a main driver of the country's economic growth. In 2010, China's service industry accounted for 43.1% of the country's GDP, which was well below the developed countries' average level of about 70% (National Bureau of Statistics of China 2011). China's service industry continues to lag behind other sectors, only accounting for a small portion of the national economy. The production-related and livelihood-related industrial sectors serve the large market demand and offer exceptional growth potential.

With their active involvement and participation in the international business society, well-known Chinese corporations are realising the importance of investing in sustainable and responsible development. They are proactively promoting and sponsoring public interest programmes such as environmental protection, poverty aid, education development and food safety. Stated another way, the value proposition of social responsibility and sustainability is increasingly essential for industry leaders who desire to introduce their business innovation, and as a result, industrial service design is expected to play an important role in the entire innovation process, emphasising the concepts and methods applied.

This chapter will introduce the context of the growing industrial service design in China, and two cases will be discussed to show how tools can be used to adopt a system perspective, deal with multiple stakeholders and, most importantly, understand customers' needs, desires and habits, with the aim to deliver the best possible experience.

Growing industrial service design in China

Industrial service design has started to play a more meaningful role in China's industrial transformation, helping to improve quality and efficiency, customer-service experience and social entrepreneurship by solving hard and soft problems related to innovation and creation. Industrialisation requires both the development of industries and the development of the service sector. Service design requires 'a deep understanding and respect for human behaviors, attitudes, dreams and capacities as the essential premise for any design action' (Meroni and Sangiorgi 2011: 203). Service design has been applied as a holistic and comprehensive solution, enabling more active intervention in economic and social life intended to bring about positive changes.

China is likely to see industrial entrepreneurship rise significantly in the near future. This will be driven by the large population, the growing number of young people with a business education and the Government's increasing acceptance and support of independent start-up businesses. Although the next potential market for industrial service design will be in traditional industries, the current milestones and remarkable performance of industrial service design has been rooted in high-tech industries. By using analytical problem-solving design tools, industrial service design has shown its effectiveness in the following aspects:

Branding differentiation and precise marketing

Typical example: Xiaomi Technology, the world's third-largest smartphone maker. Xiaomi designs, develops and sells smartphones, smart home products, mobile apps and related consumer electronics. Xiaomi's innovative business model has been characterised as a disruptive force in the existing smartphone industry by a number of commentators. Xiaomi's target consumers are the young population of China, especially college students and young adults who have just entered the workforce. As they get places of their own, these young people need TVs, air purifiers and so on; things that Xiaomi sells along with smartphones. Industrial service design, in line with this marketing strategy, led to the introduction of a new Internet-only selling channel. Xiaomi does not own a single physical store, selling its products exclusively from its own online store instead. The company also did away with traditional advertising and relies on social-networking services, as well as its own customers to help advertise its products.

Service quality and customer experience improvement

Typical example: JD.com, one of the largest business-to-customer (B2C) online retailers in China based on transaction volume. The company strives to offer consumers the best online shopping experience. Through its content-rich and user-friendly website and mobile applications, JD.com offers a wide selection of products at competitive prices and delivers those products in a speedy and reliable manner. Satisfaction with its delivery service is based largely on the company's competition strategy. Alibaba is the largest online e-commerce platform in China. However, rather than follow Alibaba's model of outsourcing to third-party suppliers, JD.com designed and then invested in highly automated warehousing systems in two Chinese cities, to provide same-day and next-day delivery via the last-mile delivery network, even during peak periods.

Online service capability establishment

Typical example: Meituan and Dianping, a Chinese Yelp-like local review and Groupon-like group-buying service provider with a strong focus on restaurants. The merged company has a combined share of more than 80% of China's online-to-offline (O2O) services group-buying market, which involves collaboration between websites and restaurants. With the rapid development of mobile Internet, China's strong consumption market attracted tens of thousands of entrepreneurs looking to ride the mobile Internet start-up wave, particularly in the O2O sector. Led by social media, in-store omni-channel commerce and mobile technologies, the digital revolution is continuing and expanding, forcing brands and retailers to adapt their plans and develop new market solutions. Industrial service design must strike a balance between technology and convenience, leveraging cutting-edge technical capabilities and creating service coverage that is as broad as possible via mobile Internet.

Service design for the largest charity organisation in China: case study of One Foundation

Taking these aspects into account from the beginning of the design process results in more effective solutions, not only for the corporate world but also for the social-innovation world, where stakeholder engagement and empathy with users are crucial to the successful implementation of solutions, even if those products consist of a single product. This proved to be true with several projects developed by Yang Design for One Foundation, the largest charity organisation in China, which specialises in disaster relief and childcare.

It started out as a straightforward product design project: the team had to take a field trip to Ya'an, one of the areas hit by the Lushan earthquake in 2013. There, the team intended to study issues with the existing tents, based on common military designs, and design a better version. However, when the team arrived, they immediately realised that the project was much more complex than it had appeared. First, there were many practical issues the earthquake victims had to deal with: from managing cables to using additional roof fabric to avoid rainwater leaks. The most important consideration, however, was the deep emotional needs of the victims. For instance, the team noticed that people were attempting to create extra outdoor space by connecting several tents together. The designers initially thought this was due to a lack of indoor space, but there was more to the story: families wanted to rebuild a sense of community, restore their lost neighbourhoods, recreate meeting places and connect to their neighbours and family members.

Another important realisation was the fact that victims were not the only ones involved with the tents: there were many other stakeholders, such as volunteers and camp managers, who also had many insights to share; for example, the lack of a clear way to number the tents and designate their inhabitants. The designers realised that to create a truly better tent, they had to learn to empathise with the victims, while also enlarging their perspective to consider the whole life cycle of the tent, as well as all involved stakeholders. Thus, the team decided to borrow the ways of thinking and methodologies of service design to explore these issues in depth. The most relevant tools employed were:

- Stakeholder maps that highlighted each actor's needs, expectations and relationship with the relief tents.
- A 'Day in the Life' and contextual interviews, which yielded tangible information about victims' lives and issues (the team also experienced sleeping inside the tents for a few nights to empathise better with the victims).
- Co-creation workshops aimed at collecting or validating ideas directly from victims, volunteers and camp managers.
- Personas that summed up the key characteristics, needs and desires of different stakeholders.

Thanks to this system and a user-centred approach, the team was able to develop several innovative yet practical solutions. A few examples:

Owing to privacy issues, people preferred to keep their windows closed, but this caused poor ventilation and illumination as the original blue fabric flooded the tent with an eerie blue light. The issue was solved by designing transparent areas on the roof and by replacing blue fabric with light green fabric, which was chosen for its relaxing effect, its similarity to energising spring colours and its good match with the countryside environment.

Most tents were perceived to be too weak to withstand rain and wind, and so they were often covered with additional fabric layers for further protection.

This was solved by creating an extra white fabric roof, which provided better protection without compromising illumination.

The lack of space forced people to perform several activities outside their tents, such as washing clothes or socialising. This resulted in the creation of a built-in system to connect different tents together and even the inclusion of additional material to create a 'veranda' that claimed additional space.

Last but not least, volunteers and camp managers benefitted from increased ease of assembly/disassembly, and the possibility of embedding a label to allow easy identification of each family.

The combination of these features with an elegant yet affordable design resulted in Yang Design winning the International Design Excellence Award (IDEA) 2015 for this project. This led the studio to employ a similar approach in all subsequent social-innovation projects, such as the 'Onederland' playground, which was also developed for One Foundation. Thus far the results of projects have been very promising and seem to confirm the value of the service design approach and methodologies to social-innovation projects, even when the final outcome is a product. These methodologies allow designers to develop solutions that are more effective and relevant, both to the end users and to the entire system of stakeholders related to the product to be designed.

Figure 6.1 One Foundation: service design project for the company, society and social responsibility.

Service design for economic model innovation

Design Harvests' design-driven innovation, a service prototype, as well as a new kind of economic model, has been developed to practise design-driven innovation. It was founded in Xinqiao on Chongming Island, a rural location near the international city of Shanghai, as a designer-driven service innovation connecting urban and rural areas. Design-driven innovations have generated products, services and systems with long lives, significant and sustainable profit margins and brand value, and they have spurred company growth (Verganti 2009). The aim of Design Harvests is to build new developing service prototypes through 'design thinking' to facilitate the development of the environment, economy, culture and other social elements. This project illustrates that designers have adjusted their perspective and stand on a higher level to observe the world. Rice was chosen as the target of the project because it is the basic element in the food structure of southern China, and because the rural area on Chongming Island supplies farm products to the city of Shanghai. A practice was established to grow rice in a totally natural way, unlike the process in industrial agricultural production, and to promote the organic style and identity of the village by branding the design and organising activities. At the same time, local farmers were encouraged to use their agricultural wisdom to communicate with citizens and attract visitors from the city who wanted to visit a rural place and obtain more knowledge about nature.

Design has shifted in focus from tangible design to intangible design, such as service design, information design and system design (Mager 2009; Manzini 2009; Sanders 2006; Yongqi 2010). Design Harvests is a progressive experiment, and its exploration demonstrates the value in design. Designers have many identities when involved in service design. They are likely to be directors who arrange the application of social resources; they are also organisers, harmonising relationships or creating connections among diverse stakeholders; they may be entrepreneurs, managing the commercial aspects to earn financial profits with which to operate the system; and of course, they serve in the role of implementers in design projects. Designers have an important contribution to make to the worldwide movement of restorative, solidarity economy: life, not money (and not technology), is the ultimate value (Thackara 2013). The designer – and the design career itself – is updating rapidly and dramatically, which encourages designers to be pioneers, leading the whole society to consider and explore the future of social development.

The service system put forward by designers in Design Harvests is an attempt to reuse and properly utilise limited resources, and the designers participated in the entire process. Design does not raise simply top-down proposals but underlines the changing social matrix, which offers an effective promotion during this process. The role of coordinator is a significant addition to the responsibility of designers (Yongqi 2010). Apart from designing, which is their primary duty, the designers contributed to the building construction of deserted homes and helped home-owners manage the innovation hub with new commercial methods. These innovation hubs extract rural capacity with design and creativity based on potential local resources. They provide the city with products and services, and more importantly, incubate and demonstrate new economic models with the ability to stimulate employment and absorb urban intelligence, capital and resources into the country's entrepreneurship to improve interaction with local communities (Yongqi 2010). In this case, the designer plays a role in the system, as a user similar to a farmer or consumer, which allows designers to approach and receive timely feedback. When designers work like local farmers or craftsmen, they are applying the design tool of role-play, and are thus able to obtain real agricultural knowledge in the field, and inspiration regarding solutions to social issues. This is a meaningful harvest for the designers themselves.

Thanks to advanced technologies represented by the Internet, unprecedented opportunities have been provided for closed connection and vivid interaction between cities and countries. Working with a palette of characteristics – small, local, open and connected – designers create an innovation network, bringing technologies, professional knowledge and financial inputs from an urban area to a rural area, and applying the natural and space resources of the countryside. Gradually, more commercial cooperation can be achieved in rural areas, causing the countryside to become a magnet that attracts youth to return and begin entrepreneurial pursuits. Based on this kind of development tendency, Design Harvests is exploring a future morphology in a new service industry in the context of urbanisation.

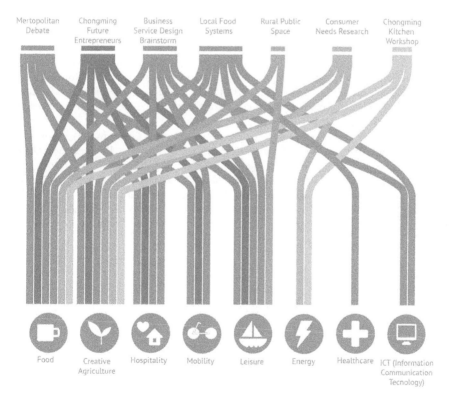

Figure 6.2 Design Harvests: service design practices for economic model innovations guided by the designers.

Conclusion

In China, service design cannot only promote innovation for economic development and business models, but can also help to solve and balance the painful issues in social transformation. The service designer should have a deep understanding of and respect for Chinese culture and history to maximise user participation and co-creation. Raising awareness of service design within other NGOs, the public and, most importantly, the Government and the industrial sector is important. Once these stakeholders understand what service design means and the value it can bring, there will be a real demand for it. The major trends in the design of future industrial service should be: more systematic methodology and service design tools; service designed to expand industry penetration, environmental protection, culture and quality of life; the connection of Big Data and information technology; and a balance between serving individuals and the public.

References

Keqiang, L. (2015) China unveils targets for 2015: Li Keqiang's speech as it happened. *South China Morning Post*, 5 March 2015.

Mager, B. (2009) Service design as an emerging field. In: Miettinen, S. and Koivisto, M. (Eds.), *Designing Services with Innovative Methods* (pp. 28–43). Helsinki: TAIK.

Manzini, E. (2009) DESIS-International: A network on Design for Social Innovation and Sustainability, Internal document. Dis-Design. Milan: Politecnico di Milano.

Meroni, A. and Sangiorgi, D. (2011) *Design for Services*. Aldershot, UK: Gower.

National Bureau of Statistics of China (2011) *China Statistical Yearbook*. China Statistics Press. Retrieved from www.stats.gov.cn/tjsj/ndsj/2011/indexeh.htm (accessed 10 January 2015).

Sanders, E. (2006) Design research in 2006. *Design Research Quarterly*, 1(1), pp. 4–8.

Thackara, J. (2013) *Design for a Restorative Economy. Design Harvests: An Acupunctural Design Approach Towards Sustainability*. Gothenburg: Mistra Urban Futures.

Verganti, R. (2009) *Design Driven Innovation Changing the Rules of Competition by Radically Innovating What Things Mean*. Boston, MA: Harvard Business Press.

Yongqi, L. (2010) An acupunctural sustainable design approach: Strategic design of Chongming Xiaoqiao sustainable community. *Creation and Design*, 4, pp. 33–38.

Part III

Hands-on industrial service design

Designers talking about industrial service design

7   New eyes on value creation
Case study: Tetra Pak

Marcus Gabrielsson and Malin Orebäck

Keywords: Tetra Pak, Veryday, front-end innovation, business case, New Eyes approach, innovation process

We love peeking inside cupboards. That is what service designers do. But we also take a hard look at the business case behind what we find there. Check inside your own kitchen cabinets. Chances are they are stocked with a few of the more than 179 billion Tetra Pak cartons that bring food products to consumers around the world each year.[1] In a large industrial organisation like Tetra Pak, even a small engineering change can have a huge impact along the entire value chain. But innovation is not just about producing a better physical product. Deep insights about stakeholder needs help businesses fill knowledge gaps, identify intangible opportunities and connect with the partners and customers they would like to reach or serve better.

The New Eyes assignment

Tetra Pak asked Veryday to join with their front-end innovation (FEI) team to explore the value chain with 'new eyes'. Our shared goal was to come up with solid innovation opportunities based on service-design thinking, creative business models and strong business cases. We approached the project with a set of research methods that offer great value to traditional industrial companies operating in large ecosystems. We saw ourselves as a small speedboat making exploratory runs for a huge ship, looking for clear channels and new routes that would move the big boat along to uncharted, or perhaps undiscovered, territories. Throughout the engagement, the FEI and Veryday teams manned the speedboat together.

Tetra Pak presented an assignment that service designers dream about: there were no silos to steer around. Our mandate was to create concepts horizontally across the value chain, in effect sifting through all the silos – and to bring numbers into the equation, too. The New Eyes research targeted a specific line of aseptic packaging and encouraged exploration into retail, Big Data, tracking, consumer needs, customer value and any other area or form that a new opportunity could possibly take.

Karin Marcovecchio, Lead User Experience Researcher at Tetra Pak, explains the structure of FEI within the Tetra Pak organisation: 'We're quite a new constellation of people ... discovery and venture is quite a new way of working', referring to how a discovery project out of FEI can potentially launch a future market test, venture or prototype. Unbound by conventional industrial development processes or timelines, FEI's mandate is to infuse the organisation with new ideas and plant seeds that may germinate in ten to fifteen years' time. Or, as Marcovecchio describes, 'it's bubbling, like sourdough, slowly rising'.

During the summer of 2015, for example, the time was right for a Tetra Pak venture that developed out of an FEI discovery from a few years ago. The new concept bundled portion packages into a 3-pack, and then placed them directly next to the current retail solution (same brand and product) in several retailers in Lund, Malmö and Stockholm, Sweden. On average, the new 3-pack sold 50 per cent more than the original solution. Marcovecchio observes that this type of small market test is 'one way of trying to sell a soft value within the organization', and illustrates how the FEI model delivers through less traditional channels.

Enter service design

Over a seven-month period, we searched for the unmet and underserved needs of stakeholders in two market areas targeted by Tetra Pak: China and Brazil. Based on stakeholder mapping, qualitative conversations were conducted with 113 respondents, including internal experts, customers, distributors, retailers and consumers. Thirty-two insight themes were generated based on important discoveries from one or both markets, and then 22 larger opportunity areas were identified and detailed. Ultimately, five concepts were selected to fully develop and quantify with specific business cases. In the allotted time frame, it was a feat of massive scale.

This way of working – including the business case as an integral part of the service-design process *and* across a large part of the value chain – was unique in our experience, and it was the first time we witnessed a project become so smart so quickly. Encouraged by FEI, we thought outside the box, put our thinking into a new box and then thought outside of that box.

Marcovecchio notes that FEI is 'supposed to challenge a bit, or give new ideas and suggestions', and from a front-end perspective, the distinct framework achieved positive outcomes. Tetra Pak also recognised the complexity of the New Eyes methodology and its impact scenarios.

Some of the industrial organisations and government entities Veryday has worked with previously have been quite comfortable with precise, engineering-driven innovation and the traditional development process that launches a service-design project from one particular marketing, sales or research and development (R&D) silo. The traditional process is either revenue-driven, so the numbers rule (although it may offer less potential for delivering true user value), or it is developed from the bottom-up by user needs and does not necessarily have an optimal financial impact. These stakeholders may find it challenging to relate to the value of the New Eyes approach.

However, the process used in the Tetra Pak engagement bridged this gap and created value because the impact scenarios were anchored on a stable tripod: concept + narrative + business case. Areas of overlap that proved value, both financially and throughout the entire value chain, were identified. The objective to deliver both business value *and* compelling reasons to launch a venture based on credible quantitative and user data was met.

Building the business case

In a classic service-design challenge, we look for user needs and create solutions around them. However, even the most visionary ideas may end up in a drawer if they cannot be quantified by solid numbers.

Common service-design practice makes research robust through quantitative data. Instead, Veryday uses qualitative techniques to create a solid foundation for building valuable solutions, and then we make research robust through the business case.

In New Eyes, the tripod approach examined financial opportunities as creatively as a design strategist or service designer explores user-need opportunities. Propositions were built that would add value based on customer, distributor, retailer and consumer needs, and potential impacts were examined based on what logistics, R&D, data and other business areas inside and outside the organisation might require. 'We also looked at data from the marketing side of Tetra Pak. We interviewed a lot of people that have been working in the markets and market companies targeted in the New Eyes project', observed Marcovecchio.

Before the financial team sat down to calculate each business case, related business models were built using a design approach that concretely described potential value streams in a new way. By creatively prototyping, mapping and iterating, we physically showed areas that could contribute to revenue, where costs might occur and which players might be prepared to pay for a particular benefit.

The work integrated user and business values concurrently as opposed to sequentially, and it quickly evolved into a rich innovation approach. As Magnus Hedenström, Partner and Founder of Cupole Consulting Group, and Veryday's partner in creating the New Eyes business models and business cases, observes: 'My key takeaway from the project is the value of combining deep research and insights with financial business analysis to create a robust platform for cross-functional breakthrough innovation work, bringing the organization and key stakeholders together in the process.'

Methodology, process and tools

New Eyes employed four phases of the Veryday 'proven innovation process': internal exploration; discovery; opportunity mapping; and impact scenario.

The decision to include stakeholders in research, analysis, concept ideation and business-case generation was another way the speedboat traversed the entire value chain. From day one, we worked together closely to ensure that the end results were valuable to Tetra Pak and to as many external entities as could be identified.

'What we did on the consumer and the customer exploration side was to look for the needs, problems and areas where we could actually create a solution', Marcovecchio notes.

A single mother we talked with in Sao Paolo described how frozen broccoli turned out to be the one food that satisfied both her need to provide safe, healthy food for her eight-year-old son and his need for food he enjoyed and found fun to eat. Uncovering consumer tensions like these in our research can be the catalyst for brands and consumers to partner on common goals, create new services and pursue fresh opportunities.

Internal exploration

Workshops at home with key stakeholders defined scope and established a common knowledge level. Brazil and China were selected as key markets, in part for their size and also because they represent challenging markets.

Marcovecchio recalls that internal exploration 'started half a year before we even contacted Veryday. We did quite extensive work and I think that was important for selling it to the organization.'

Discovery

In the field, the crossover team conducted in-depth interviews with representatives from all parts of the value chain. We also worked with experience prototyping and used a transformative new method. As consumers presented the concepts they had developed, we took smartphone videos and edited the most productive sessions right on the spot. These podcasts were quickly sent along to interviewers who were conducting sessions with customers, distributors and retailers. This insight/prototype relay injected consumer stories into another context and allowed respondents to immediately reflect and build on a concept. The process jumped between parallel streams and generated feedback rapidly.

In our multi-methodology set-up, we co-create a lot. We come to interviews armed with a set of tools for an array of potential conversations, so if one framework does not suit a particular individual, we can put it aside and try another approach. We bring along props and ask people to build something, draw something or move things around to physically explain their emotions and what they are trying to express in a more tactile manner.

'What I think was especially smart with this research was that we used so many different techniques', says Marcovecchio. The tools enabled consumers to express their feelings. FEI trusted the exploratory nature of the process and our sense of when to follow the tracks of a story that appeared out of nowhere.

While it is daring to go off-script, over time service designers instinctively learn when to step away and see what takes off.

New Eyes delivered one of the highest quality research sets ever produced by Veryday. Marcovecchio agrees: 'It's always interesting to go out in the market. I think it was a great discovery. We learned a lot.'

Opportunity mapping

Immediately upon completing fieldwork, the extended team collaborated on an open-door analysis. 'To arrive at the insights, we crashed into all these small Post-It notes as soon as we came home. We haven't always been a part of that process. It's quite chaotic, but fun', observes Marcovecchio.

Opportunity mapping began by rotating large boards, that each covered four insights, around to the multi-stakeholder teams. Marcovecchio recalls that there was:

> one person from the China research and one from the Brazil research on each team. We took a solid amount of time to go through the insight material together, which made it quite easy to build opportunities upon the insights and make connections between them.

Impact scenario

In the last phase, we identified the business opportunities that would become the final deliverables. Comprised of concept + narrative + business case, these impact scenarios were brought to life through videos that conveyed the complete storytelling behind each scenario.

The *concept* describes the opportunity, competition, target market, revenue model, feasibility and value proposition – and how it works.

The *narrative* connects each opportunity with trend work and the insights uncovered during in-depth conversations with people in the market. These 'red thread' scenarios are the missing link that anchors fiscal stories with real human needs.

The *business case* is the potential business impact based on a number of well-considered evaluations made by financial teams. What will be the biggest trend to look at in ten years' time? Will it be profitable from day one or take longer to capture revenue? What is the break-even time frame? Can the idea be legally protected? Can it stand alone in the market? All these factors result in an overall opportunity score.

Conclusion

Large industrial organisations may find it challenging to move forward and meet stakeholder needs that extend beyond new products and product development, especially if they are comfortable with the standard industrial model, which tends to focus on technological innovation within silos.

These companies often see concepts that have a business case attached to them but are missing a narrative – the red thread that anchors numbers in real needs. The goal of the New Eyes engagement was to extend the focus beyond a single silo and link multiple stakeholders holistically, through research, analysis, concept generation, revenue analysis and other activities. By merging user rules and number rules, we built overall stronger opportunities that included as many parts of the value chain as possible.

We looked through cupboards in the suburbs of Shanghai, Chengdu and Sao Paolo with our FEI partners, and clients often remember this type of fieldwork long after an engagement wraps up. These are the nitty-gritty details that create internal advocates for ideas in the longer term, and ultimately, influence an organisation in a way that cold, hard numbers alone cannot. In a recent conversation with Karin Marcovecchio about takeaways from the New Eyes project, we kept coming back to the many human factors in the service-design process. She concludes that ultimately 'you cannot really argue with the insights'.

As service designers, we could not agree more.

Note

1 www.tetrapak.com/us/about/short-facts.

8 Service innovation at Volkswagen

Putting services into the core of the business

Marianna Recchia and Julia Kleeberger

Keywords: Volkswagen, pilot, case study, business case, user-centred design

Back in 2012, Marianna and Julia had the chance to work together at Volkswagen Group Research as part of a young team with mixed professional backgrounds (business, service design, UX). Bringing a fresh mindset to the company culture, they started to run projects with the aim of testing new offers around the core business and challenging the existing product-development processes. They used a co-creation approach to involve colleagues from different departments during the early stages of their projects and highlighted the importance of receiving customer feedback throughout the design process. They tried to adapt Service Design Tools to the everyday practices of VW Financial Services, IT and Marketing, and came up with hybrid methods that might sound familiar to those speaking different languages inside the company.

Based on their experiences of working in the Service Innovation Team at Volkswagen Research, in this chapter Marianna and Julia discuss their successes and failures in fronting the company's challenges, as well as the knowledge they gained from reflecting on the cultural influence those projects had on the company.

How did service innovation develop at Volkswagen?

Service innovation at Volkswagen developed within the research department. This might seem a bit unusual as the design and marketing departments have sovereignty over the customer, as well as a holistic mindset to approach challenges. However, in research you find the freedom for exploration and failing alongside a need for innovative solutions, which are crucial for the development of new methods and ways of working.

Before beginning service-design projects, the research department was mainly technically driven. Despite having highly skilled usability, research among the Volkswagen colleagues focused mainly on enhancing the usability of the product rather than concentrating on customer needs and desires from the beginning of the project. User-centred design approaches played almost no role.

There were a few young minds with design and human-centred backgrounds among the engineers, so new ideas were developed for finding solutions to upcoming challenges in the automobile sector, and thus the service innovation team was founded. While producing the first results and always visualising and showing them, whether they were based on customer insights, concept ideas or first-use cases, the power of service-design thinking became apparent to those higher in the hierarchy and success followed.

With only limited initial resources, working with universities such as Aalto University, Köln International School of Design (KISD), Germany, or Savannah College of Art and Design (SCAD), in the USA, helped us to quickly ramp up their knowledge and generate convincing results.

However, in meetings to push our results further, we often observed that our dialogue partners realised the potential of the results but had no way to integrate them into their daily business. This became particularly obvious when we tried to set up project pilots. We quickly realised that the biggest part of our task would be building bridges to link the design thinking methods to the Volkswagen organisation.

Case study

To illustrate the challenges we faced, we would like to describe in more detail our efforts to set up a pilot. The challenge of the project was to take an existing concept previously developed by the team, in collaboration with the financial services department, and plan a test phase with an increasing number of customers. The aim was to verify the attractiveness of the concept as a new offer for the customer and as a new business model for the company. The decision to test a digital financial service instead of a new car feature was guided by the need to move beyond the company's classic product-development processes, as well as the need to show the potential of products traditionally considered secondary cross-selling opportunities but not as independent, profitable business cases. The service was thought of as a way to make a typical 'cost of ownership' service (e.g. fuelling) less painful, and even more interactive and attractive for the customer.

Our first steps towards the definition of a 'minimum viable product' were:

- Scanning the results of the market and user research that led to the concept prototypes, to understand which insights were included in those first releases and which were assumed to be less relevant.
- Interviewing the internal people involved in the design of the concept, to compare their different perspectives on its 'unique selling point', and on the success factors that would define its chance to go on the market.
- 'Deconstructing' the concept to identify the main features of the product, prioritising the ones worthy of being tested according to our scope and budget, and combining them again in a new prototype.
- Collecting feedback on the new prototype from internal and external experts in the product area to get opinions on 'why, how and to whom would you sell this product?' in order to create a detailed stakeholder map with criticisms and expectations.

- Conducting a quantitative study to test different product scenarios in order to choose the price models to be tested and to identify the screening criteria for the test candidates.

The preparation of the pilot consisted of:

- Creating a pilot team, which was supported throughout the process by the University of Brunswick and a lean digital service agency.
- Developing the beta version of the product: a front- and back-end price-calculation tool.
- Designing a suitable test process, methods and tools: iteration phases, selection of metrics and goals, database documentation, analytics, workshop materials, surveys and interview scripts for the testers.
- Participating directly in the selection of the testers, presenting the product to them and trying to answer their initial questions.

Two pilot phases were conducted:

- Six months with 50 customers living in an urban region.
- Six months with a sample of 300 customers living in urban and country regions.

The collected results converged in:

- Business case and scenario analysis, with alternative assumptions about time to market and time to profit.
- Requirements analysis for the further development of the product: audit of existing company functions, systems and resources, as well as future investments, outsourcing and partnership opportunities.
- Strategic vision for the creation of a new market for Volkswagen's digital services.

What we learned

In sum, one of the most crucial things for running a successful pilot for us was the ability to modify our assumptions and our idea of the product continuously. Not sticking with the first solution but rather creating several new product releases during the test phase helped us learn about the service offer, the changing behaviour of our customers and the power and influence of promotional actions to modify their attitude.

Additionally, after the first three months of the pilot, we invited our best ten customers to a dinner at which we could all exchange ideas about the product experience. This helped us to develop a deeper understanding of the needs and wants of our customers and also further boosted our empathy. The direct relationship with the customer was a huge motivator for the whole team to work eagerly on the refinement. Moreover, the direct contact also supported the building of trust between customers and all the people involved in the service, including the product owners, first- and second-level support and employees of our partner fuel stations, who became valuable supporters of the project.

Running the pilot and thus making results tangible also informed important decision-making with regard to adopting or killing the product for the departments involved. Furthermore, while only being at the test phase, the discussions about integrating the service and the new business into their product portfolio and development processes made everything concrete, which motivated the search for solutions and sped up the whole process.

Finally, running the pilot also improved our understanding of the required costs, time and resources of everyday business.

Progression

After two years of intense work, we accumulated lots of experiences. One of the major insights we gained was that living up to a culture of failure and iterative learning from mistakes was hard to establish in the mindsets of our colleagues, who believed in a brand that stands for high-quality cars that experience no failures.

It became obvious that arguing about customer satisfaction obtained through a human-centred approach would not be enough; it was necessary to quantify the cost savings and additional revenues. This led to the consequent decision to extend the skill set and activity portfolio of the team. Adding new employees skilled in strategic design and business-case analysis, who worked more closely with experts from the financial department and from other technical departments of the group, we improved our capacity to strengthen the viability and feasibility of our concepts. The team was originally no more than an experimental unit of open-minded people who wanted to do something disruptive, but it became a valid internal partner in the evolution of the current business. Much effort was given to exploring new pricing models, direct/indirect revenue schemes and new metrics, to describe and validate digital service business opportunities. These opportunities were picked up from the big thematic areas of the Internet of Things, automatic driving and intelligent mobility.

Thus, on the one hand, we worked on extending our design approach from business ideation to business-case calculation. On the other hand, we spent time documenting the methods we used, and creating tools that could be used by other departments within the company.

We also put more effort into our networking activities. As we frequently ran networking meet-ups in order to connect with colleagues from different departments and support the watering down of the silo-thinking mentality, we now decided to do this in a more professional way. Thus, we set up an in-house business-innovation conference, targeting all the people who had contact with us in their daily business. External speakers were invited, and interactive workshop sessions were held where people could work together on new and existing concepts, using different business model prototyping techniques. The conference was a great success in terms of networking, and it helped to expand the mindsets of the participants.

In expanding the portfolio and putting effort into networking, the team became a valuable dialogue partner for business issues, while remaining designers and approaching challenges with a holistic mindset.

Our personal view

After being part of the service innovation team for over three years, in the autumn of 2015, Marianna decided to move to the IT department that implements the connected car services. Her decision was motivated by a curiosity to test how service and UX design would combine with requirement engineering. She is not a pioneer in this; the service-design discipline has already made important contributions in this field. Marianna is very grateful to all the researchers who are unknowingly helping her to find an orientation between architecture and system specifications. Her big dream is to one day write something worthy to be read in the field of system design, but in the meantime she organises user research and tests to show their value in the latest stages of product development and product management. Marianna says: 'Hey, we are not so different; I do blueprints too!'

Looking ahead, Julia realised that even the initiated changes would not be enough. The world is facing huge problems such as climate change, overpopulation and shortages of health care, food and energy. Thus, to connect effectively with people and create meaningful ecosystems, businesses need to understand what creates meaning for people and how they can connect to global problems. Therefore, it is important to connect internal teams with outside experts. The corporate teams' tasks will shift from developing new mobility services to orchestrating experts from different fields and, with the help of knowledge about the internal culture, to building bridges into the company, thus enabling social transformation. To support and accelerate this transformation process, the tools and methods used in design thinking should be employed.

The first outcome of Julia's work was the foundation of *Junge Tüftler*, an organisation that teaches children digital literacy using a constructionist approach. Through this organisation, she helps children develop the mental models and skill sets they need to grow up as engaged citizens with twenty-first-century skills and, hopefully, become the change-makers of tomorrow.

Conclusion

Having established a successful link between concept development and piloting and transferring services, it became obvious that moving towards the development and integration of mobility services in our core business seemed to be the best action.

Looking back, working in an R&D department gave us the opportunity to explore and try new things without being affected by classic big-company phenomena like poor culture or placing no value on good customer experiences. However, in comparison to other automotive R&D projects, services cannot be easily transferred to the engineering department. Additionally, because we were a small team in a research department, we had a limited budget and resources to design and pilot a number of concepts per year, and scale our experiments. Our company supported our activities, but we struggled to create a standardised process to implement innovation. Owing to organisational shortcomings, we had problems scaling our results and suggesting new implementation and operation paths for our projects.

Therefore, it is important to include service innovation at the core of the business. We view the five years of intense experiments and team changes as the foundation for a new phase in which service design can play a strong role in enhancing the integration of this new paradigm in the company's daily business and consolidated processes.

Considering the recent transformations within the Volkswagen Group, we have a chance to include the topic of servitisation in the Group's strategic innovation roadmap. In doing so, the service-design discipline will evolve from testing out new services and possibilities for Volkswagen into defining holistic service-economy systems and, thus, being able to influence a company's entire business strategy.

Other innovation initiatives have been taken and new teams working with agile and design-thinking methods have been created at our headquarters and in our brands. It would be impossible to succeed without a network that spreads ideas and good practices and exchanges resources.

Your organisation needs empathetic people who can adapt easily to circumstances within the organisation, are open-minded regarding new topics and ways of working and are eager to learn to face the upcoming challenges. Additionally, when performing service innovation in an industry context, you need to be able to adapt to upcoming changes and developments within the company and its culture on one hand, and to the quickly changing external environment on the other. Therefore, it is important to always have new players, competitors and potential business partners in your scope.

References

Buxton, B. (2010) *Sketching User Experiences: Getting the Design Right and the Right Design.* San Francisco: Morgan Kaufmann.

Den Ouden, E. (2011) *Innovation Design: Creating Value for People, Organizations and Society.* London, Dordrecht: Springer Science & Business Media.

Miettinen, S. and Valtonen, A. (2013) *Service Design with Theory: Discussions on Change, Value and Methods.* Rovaniemi: Lapland University Press.

Osterwalder, A. and Pigneur, Y. (2010) *Business Model Generation: A Handbook for Visionaries, Game Changers, and Challengers.* Hoboken, NJ: John Wiley & Sons.

9 Facilitating corporate partnerships

Katrine Rau

Keywords: strategic alignment, empathy, facilitation, and visualisation

Many large organisations today include diverse stakeholders and numerous products, vendors and (sometimes conflicting) strategies. Add the notion of digital products to the equation, and speed becomes one of the biggest drivers – and biggest constraints. In today's digital world, companies need to move extremely fast, as the market evolves more quickly than products can actually be produced. This results in a situation in which even large companies need to evolve quickly with strong partners throughout the supply chain. Evolving together requires more than just strong collaboration; to form a strong partnership, it is necessary for two companies to identify overlapping opportunities at a strategic level.

Service design as a professional practice has a unique ability to accelerate development in B2B companies that rely on multiple vendors and stakeholders for success. An experienced service designer can be beneficial as a neutral facilitator when it comes to creating alignment between two partnering companies. And by involving design at earlier stages, B2B organisations increase the chance of reaching strategic alignment. The stages and the steps of this B2B service design process can result in improved communications, faster processes and stronger initiatives.

This chapter will discuss the following questions:

- What are the unique challenges that large organisations face?
- Why are service designers becoming more valuable in B2B organisations?
- What are the stages and practical steps that a service designer must take to reach strategic alignment?

Understanding the development cycle and strategic alignment

The stages and activities that are necessary for the development of a new service system, such as city-wide taxation protocols or a mobile application, are known as the development process or the development cycle. The development process ranges from line manufacturing to agile software development, and no two cycles are identical. Throughout the process, a number of stakeholders, vendors and partners can be involved to strengthen (but also complicate) the process. Even the simplest decision often requires multiple stakeholders to agree in order to advance through the development cycle (Hammer and Champy 2009).

For many years, design became involved in the development cycle near the end of the process, after much of the service system had already been created. Work performed after the strategic components of a system are already in place is 'late-stage involvement'. When involved at this late stage, the designer is often tasked with decorating the system aesthetically rather than influencing the development of the system itself. In these situations, design is more of an afterthought than a major contributor to the service itself. The notion of aesthetically decorating an inherently flawed product system or service system during the late stage of development does not take advantage of service-designers' ability to design a new way of running a profitable business.

The need for strategic alignment, or a state of agreement that serves the interests of multiple parties, appears in the beginning of initial conversations between vendors and partners. Companies have the opportunity to understand their own strategies more clearly and, sometimes, to apply a more appropriate strategy to meet the industry's needs. Creating this strategic alignment between two companies is not an easy task, especially if we are talking about large, old companies with different strategies for different departments or product lines.

There is a chance to involve service designers as neutral facilitators in the 'discovery phase', where there is a clear need for alignment.

Understanding the challenges service designers face in large organisations

The following fictionalised story is informed by public case studies about large organisations presented at Global Service Design Network conferences over the past five years.

> GloboShare Bank is a consumer bank for executives who travel more than 25% of the time. GloboShare's speciality is ensuring they can support their travelling customers in every major city in the world. GloboShare intends to release a line of attractive, robust ATMs in 15 major cities, in order to attract new customers and serve current customers. Historically, GloboShare has not owned their ATMs. Instead, each customer has an electronic bank card that works anywhere in the world. The executives at GloboShare ask representatives from across the country to form a committee responsible for releasing ATMs in the following year. The members of this committee include marketing managers and representatives from different teams in the company, such as digital security, visual identity and research and development (R&D).

Large organisations such as the fictional GloboShare face unique challenges when developing new services and products. Large organisations have many diverse stakeholders and divisions, making profitable collaboration challenging. The execution of a new service often requires coordination with members of various departments within an organisation, including, but not limited to, marketing, finance, legal and corporate strategy. Each of these divisions often have unique success metrics and separate budgets. While this separation is beneficial for leaders who want to evaluate and run separate parts of the business, it interferes with an organisation's ability to align a single vision or strategy. It is this challenge that creates the need for professionals who can manage change.

As a result of different success metrics, large organisations may develop strategies that conflict with each other. When an organisation includes multiple departments, those departments will often design strategies for accomplishing their unique goals. As a result, the strategy of one department, such as R&D, may be in conflict with that of another department, such as marketing.

Large organisations often have many products or services, making management challenging. Managing the current product or service offerings within a large organisation is often the responsibility of departments. More products and services often means more time and focus on organising development efforts for them. As a result, fewer people within the organisation are capable of overseeing all of the details.

Large organisations work with many vendors, so ensuring cohesiveness across vendor contributions is challenging. It is prohibitively more expensive for a single large organisation to integrate all the competencies necessary for their full-time employees. Instead, large organisations could outsource specialists, consultants and other vendors to support their respective stages of development. For example, large organisations often retain the services of shipping centres and marketing consultants, but fewer organisations oversee how two vendors work together to create the best delivery experience possible. As a result of this vendor diversity, large organisations can reduce costs and increase the quality of parts of their operation. However, vendor diversity invites a new challenge: when hundreds of different companies who are not close to each other are all contributing to the success of one product, how can an organisation ensure that the resulting product experience is cohesive and effective?

Most large organisations have a relatively short history of producing digital products. In comparison to physical product or service development, digital development is a relatively new field. To perform competitively in the digital product market, large organisations must work faster and with more agility to design, develop, release and maintain services. The digital product market is evolving more quickly than products can actually be produced. As a result, the professionals who create these products are constantly revisiting and improving their development cycles to accommodate new technologies, strategies and partners.

While there may be many approaches to solving organisational and development challenges, one approach that has been proven to be highly successful is integrating the design practice earlier into a development cycle. The challenges described above can be viewed as design problems, or system-level problems, and to solve these problems, organisations need to empathise with the system's users through 'design thinking'. This concept was revisited recently in the *Harvard Business Review's* November 2015 issue. One of the fundamental tools in design thinking is the 'how might we …?' question, which translates a challenge into an opportunity for improving the system. The five challenges above may be translated into this question: *How might organisations with diverse stakeholders and diverse vendors collaborate in a profitable manner to create and launch a new digital product?*

While the specific answer to this question is different for each organisation, it probably includes two key elements: strategic partnerships and process facilitation. This is where a service designer's ability to act as a neutral facilitator to support the process of creating strategic alignment among cooperating companies can be very beneficial in a business-to-business (B2B) context.

Reacting to challenges through strategic partnerships and process facilitation

To respond to these challenges successfully, large companies need to evolve their product and service-development practices to integrate new, strong partnerships throughout the early and late stages of development. One of the most valuable partners to integrate early in the development process is the service designer, who translates complex challenges into tangible visualisations and roadmaps for how organisations and departments can work together to create a specific service.

> *GloboShare will likely need to work with vendors to accomplish their goal. Executives may be considering options like outsourcing the production of their new ATMs or creating a partnership to jointly develop the entire product and service experience. But GloboShare may not know exactly how to accomplish and facilitate such a task.*

In the early stages of the development process, service designers have three distinct responsibilities: practical empathy, facilitation and visualisation.

Practical empathy

The service designer researches the needs of stakeholders, vendors and end users in order to develop a cohesive understanding of priorities to consider when developing new products.

Facilitation

The service designer facilitates meetings and interactions between stakeholders, vendors and end users to create strategic alignment between partners.

Visualisation

The service designer creates tangible visualisations of how departments will collaborate, co-create and launch new services throughout the development process. Service designers utilise design-thinking processes and methods, and are often able to successfully navigate highly complex scenarios. This is because their expertise lies in navigating the process itself, not in knowledge about specific topics. Service designers are skilled at identifying user insights and combining these insights with business objectives to create concepts, services and solutions. It is with this mindset that service designers, as facilitators, can navigate the complex, messy front-end of a development process and achieve alignment with a solution. This means that the service designer often ends up functioning as process (and often meeting) facilitators. However, it requires significant experience to facilitate large groups neutrally that may have conflicting opinions. In particular, when there is a significant number of senior leaders and high financial risks, it can be beneficial to have an equally senior (or at least highly respected) facilitator.

Stages of strategic alignment in B2B organisations

Experienced service designers can be beneficial as neutral facilitators when it comes to creating alignment between two partnering companies. Companies working in a B2B (as well as a business-to-customer, B2C) context have huge opportunities to gain from the thinking process which is an early stage of development. In this process, influential questions are raised, points of agreement are written down (not just in contracts) and design activities are utilised to clarify the need for the new product or service for users, businesses and industries. In a B2B context, the service designer's role in facilitating and visualising future partnerships includes three key stages.

1. Support early dialogues regarding strategic alliances

Developing a successful partnership is more than just ensuring strong collaboration between vendors; it is necessary for the two companies to identify overlapping opportunities starting at a strategic level. This is absolutely necessary to reach strategic alignment between cooperating companies. But first, stakeholders and vendors must start a dialogue. In this situation, the early sales meetings between two companies become more focused on the 'discovery' of a potential relationship. As the conversation changes from a sales transaction to a dialogue about opportunities, the skills needed in the conversation also change. This allows new players to be considered. The need for a neutral facilitator is evident, and this is where designers can play a key role. As opportunities start to arise in initial meetings, the designer may prepare a strategic alignment workshop between the groups. In a strategically aligned relationship, the unique goals of each party are satisfied by utilising the unique specialities of the other party and identifying a strong vision for both partners to strive towards. If the partnership opportunity is too small, or is not truly important for both companies, the partnership will most likely struggle. Thus, it is very important that the right influential stakeholders are present and that time is allocated for the messy front-end of this process. It can be tempting to rush to a solution, but there is a risk of developing a product or service that is not sustainable in the marketplace, or is not actually desired by the end users.

> *GloboShare benefits from identifying ways in which different divisions and vendors, who are incentivised differently, can be incentivised to work together in order to accomplish their unique goals. Service designers can facilitate sessions in which the stakeholders and vendors identify goals and unique offerings, and help sales team members create timelines for when and how divisions and vendors can work together.*

2. Prepare for and execute a strategic alignment workshop

In a strategic alignment workshop, stakeholders and vendors review overlapping opportunities, and prioritise the actions they may take to accomplish these goals.

To begin the process, stakeholders and service designers create opportunities for divisions and vendors to share their needs, challenges and opportunities with each other. Initially, Business A may have an idea about which problem they would like to solve, and Business B may have an idea about how its previous work or resources may benefit Business A, so this becomes the starting point for the first workshop. After mentioning the workshop's agenda, objectives and ground rules, Business A presents its view of the current landscape and the challenge they would like to focus on. Business B presents prior solutions and its current approach to solving challenges.

Next, these stakeholders and service designers identify opportunities for partnering by asking 'how might we ...?' questions. The stakeholders start identifying opportunities for partnering to solve Business A's challenge using some of Business B's methods for solving similar problems. This is where the service designer as facilitator comes into the picture. Through exercises like 'how might we ...?' a conversation is formed to identify areas of opportunity. 'How might we ...?' is an exercise that has been used in the business and design community for many years. Each opportunity is phrased as follows: 'How might we (insert opportunity)?' When all stakeholders have written down all the opportunities that they can think of, the opportunities are categorised and discussed.

Once an alignment is created, the service designer can also facilitate dialogue to identify which development initiatives should be prioritised to reach this alignment. This can result in fewer new products and services but more meaningful offerings, or, in other words, products and services that are developed by empathising with the end users. Unlike the traditional business strategy of creating a large selection of offerings in the hope that a customer will find one that fits, a design-influenced business strategy focuses on meaningful offerings.

As categories of opportunities are formed, they can be prioritised. Through this activity, the focus starts narrowing on the specifics of the challenge and opportunity. This is not easy, but through well-facilitated activities, the stakeholders can select a key partnership opportunity. It is not the facilitator's role to determine the priorities, but rather to facilitate the process of identifying priorities. In other words, if no one starts categorising the opportunities by themselves, the service designer can initiate the activity, show the stakeholders what an example of a category could be and encourage them to take part in (and eventually take over) the organising. When all the opportunities are categorised, the service designer can read the categories and introduce the activity of prioritising. Again, the service designer steps back and lets the stakeholders prioritise.

Near the end of these exercises, the stakeholders may focus on opportunities regarding target users. The dialogue can continue to dive into the specific opportunity by identifying the target user group and creating a fictional persona to represent the target user (which later on needs to be validated through user research). Creating personas is a way for the entire stakeholder group to identify with the same target user, thus gaining empathy and understanding for the needs and priorities of this user. A persona can also be used as a stepping stone to a journey map of, for example, their work process, if that is important for the project.

A workshop may continue with several other activities, depending on the objectives and time. Speed and pacing are key for the workshop. It is the facilitator's job to keep the team on track regarding objectives and time. The conversation can often go off track if the facilitator doesn't keep the dialogue focused. Before ending the workshop, it is important that all stakeholders walk away with a clear understanding of their roles and responsibilities.

> *GloboShare might invite already-established vendors to a workshop to explore opportunities for utilising their technology and existing data to better understand customers in the cities in which the new ATMs will be placed. In a facilitating role, service designers can:*
> - *Clarify the expectations of various stakeholders, divisions and vendors.*
> - *Drive a dialogue for defining strategic opportunities through workshops utilising design activities and visualisations.*
> - *Refocus development strategies to create meaningful offerings.*
> - *Clearly define the next steps for the partnership.*

3. Acting on strategic alignment

Ensuring that the momentum continues after the workshop is almost as important as facilitating the workshop itself. It can be easy for the stakeholders to lose focus of the alignment goals if they do not have a clear incentive for continuing. It will quickly become clear whether the scope of the opportunity is important enough for all stakeholders to stay engaged in the process. If that is the case, a true win–win opportunity has been found.

The ways in which teams act on strategic alignment vary based on the complexity of the service, the needs of the stakeholders and the infrastructure that is supporting the current system.

GloboShare could decide to work with a research vendor to understand the needs of the customers in the cities in which new ATMs will be placed. During this stage, service designers need to coordinate roadmaps with action plans for developing the strategic initiatives, and identify those who will be responsible for taking the next steps. Further along in the process, GloboShare might need to create a division for user research that is responsible for helping various stakeholders and divisions build empathy for each other and the end users. In this situation, service designers can integrate more user-centred practices into an organisation, such as user research departments, internal design teams and empathy-building workshops.

Conclusion

Large B2B organisations have slow, low-efficiency development cycles owing to the presence of diverse stakeholders across multiple divisions, with individual strategies that may compete with each other. Furthermore, the speed demanded by the digital market and the increased need for diverse vendors to support complex digital products results in challenges that organisations must overcome to release their offerings successfully. In response, service designers can use practical empathy, facilitation and visualisation skills early in the development cycle to bring divisions, stakeholders and vendors into a state of strategic alignment. Such strategic alignment is facilitated by the service designer, who initiates dialogues between stakeholders at the beginning of the development cycle, executes strategic alignment workshops and develops methods for acting on the agreements established during such workshops.

Reference

Hammer, M. and Champy, J. (2009) *Reengineering the Corporation: Manifesto for Business Revolution.* New York: Zondervan.

10 Co-design of change

Why changing what people do should be the key ingredient in service design

Reima Rönnholm

Keywords: Palmu, behaviour, change, customer-centric, empathy, participation

As the nature of design problems in many industries has become increasingly complex, companies now see design as a process and a tool, as well as a way to ensure the aesthetic quality of the final outcome. Managers often take courses in design thinking, and increasingly, more corporations are trying to adapt service design to make their development processes more user-centric and agile and their results more innovative (Merholz et al. 2008). Design research helps companies better understand the true needs of their customers. Co-design helps organisations develop products and services with their customers. Prototyping and a lean development culture with fast iterations help to validate new ideas earlier and steer initiatives in the right direction. However, in addition to interviewing users, mapping touchpoints and building interfaces, service designers often find themselves working with other issues inside corporations, in fields like leadership and process development, organisational change and policymaking. Consulting-related organisational change demands its own skillset, and there are a number of well-established specialists. So, can service design as an approach provide added value compared to traditional change management and consulting?

A big problem with service design today is that it focuses on talking and drawing. If you have ever been part of a service design project or seen a case study about one, you will have seen the walls full of Post-Its. When projects are presented in this way, it feels like they show pictures because they are more focused on the process and working with users rather than making long-term changes. Post-Its have not solved one problem nor made anyone's experience better; they are not the tools of change. There is a need for service design to expand from concept development to the implementation of service concepts and organisational changes. We need to move from talking and analysing to doing, and in order to take action, we need to involve the people affected by the change, as they comprise the machine running the services. Service design is about empathy. This article explores how empathy and co-design methods can help to orchestrate change and ease the implementation of new service concepts.

In services, design problems are a result of personal problems

So far, the biggest value that service design has brought to industries is a holistic approach to problem-solving. The service design process starts with customers and identifying problems, not from predefined ideas for solutions, nor from the fields in which solutions could be found. This helps industries better allocate their resources into the areas where the most value can be gained. We once did a service design project in the cleaning sector, starting with a preliminary hypothesis that value could be added to services through small gestures, such as nice messages left by cleaning staff after they finished their work. After some client and service personnel interviews, it became obvious that the real problem to be addressed was quality, and it turned out that quality-related problems were actually caused by communication problems, such as a broken phone, not by the cleaning staff. So, instead of developing smiley face stickers to place on refrigerator doors, the project turned into a leadership and communication development campaign.

Increasingly, many companies are focusing on involving customers in service development. It is no longer uncommon to talk about customers' emotions in the boardroom. However, many companies have missed the human part of the service process; that is, the employees and staff. The people who use, experience and produce services are key elements in the development of all services. However, involvement of staff in service development is rare. Typically, development work stays in a development silo and falls under the domain of a specialist. This also presents a challenge related to a holistic approach: when you start a project based purely on your customers, without understanding all the areas in the organisation that need to be included in the changes, many unexpected barriers may arise as you move forward. Some of them may be technology-related, but many are people-related. Typically, traditionally led organisations are not good at managing this kind of uncertainty.

Services come alive through interactions between people or among people, spaces and interfaces. There are few service design projects that do not lead to a need for changes in peoples' behaviour and digital touchpoints. In order to make concepts a reality, people, services, systems and their interfaces need to be 'coded' to work differently. Often, ideas seem easy on paper, and the real challenges start when they are implemented. Few war strategies, business plans and service concepts seem to survive their first contact with reality.

All service design processes should lead to change

When talking about concept implementation and change, questions arise: How much do service designers want to be part of that process? Do we have something new to offer, or should we stay behind a drawing table to avoid getting our hands dirty in organisational struggles? A colleague of mine once said that the real service design does not start until you change how the service works, and thus how people work. Many great ideas break down or change significantly during implementation. In the real world, customers and service personnel often fail to behave as expected. They do not adapt to the new model of working because they do not receive the support they need, or the shared history of organisation culture becomes an obstacle to change.

Learning from what does not work and managing changes are part of building and reshaping services. This is why service design should always focus on behavioural change. The impact of the project should also be looked at through indicators that reflect changes in behaviour. In the corporate world, this often means identifying purchasing behaviour or affecting different behaviours throughout the customers' life span. This does not happen without changes in technology and people's daily routines, which should support and complement each other. However, compared to systems, interfaces and software, humans are more difficult to 'code'. Designing for change is very different from actually helping change occur. A successful service designer has to enable behavioural change as well as concept design.

Everybody wants change, but nobody likes to change

Forward-thinking companies are learning to identify the right problems using insight tools and co-designing solutions with customers – and they are getting good at it. But when it comes to co-designing changes with staff, many companies crumble. It is surprising how typical it is for a small group of specialists to plan interventions without exposing their ideas to the people whose daily lives will be affected by the change until late in the development process. When new service concepts are finally introduced to staff, they have heard rumours about them and are prepared to oppose them. Based on our experience, this kind of top-down change is always seen as a threat.

It is totally normal to feel unease when faced with change. Even if the planned change will be beneficial, many people within the organisation cannot see the big picture and are emotionally attached to the old models. This does not mean that people are not intelligent; we act in social groups based on what is valued within the groups. Once we get used to our ways of working, we stop questioning our behaviour. We have seen this numerous times when we start to work with a new client in a new industry. As outsiders, it is easy for us to point out 'wrong' goals, indicators and values that drive everyday routines and behaviours.

Values form the basis of the culture of the whole organisation. Shared values among the management and employees create a shared culture (Schein 2004). We constantly observe what our peers do and what they are rewarded for. Then, we mimic them in an attempt to receive the same rewards. When an outsider such as a service designer comes into the organisation, empathising and understanding existing values and behaviours are essential if organisational changes are to occur. Empathy for the customers' experience is needed to design solutions at the frontline, and empathy for the employers' experience and organisational culture is needed backstage to design for change that makes a new frontline experience possible.

Change becomes easier when you are customer-oriented

At Palmu, the agency I work for, we did a study about customer-centricity in B2B companies. The study indicates that customer-centricity is only a focus in a few companies. If it is included, it is implemented at a superficial level and is only related to the frontline of customer experience. Some companies have focused on describing methods and measuring customers' experience, and others define goals based on what customers value, but there is little connection among daily operations, measurements and goals. Customer-centricity is not yet a part of entire organisations, including organisational practices, people's attitudes and ways of working. Companies should aim to be driven by customer value, not just by internal factors.

Service design projects reveal how customer-oriented organisations actually are. Companies have to decide whether they want to change, or continue as they are and just 'coat the surface'. Usually, changes are profound; you have to change shared assumptions, values and ways of working. In those situations, companies face two challenges:

1   Making changes: Changing the service frontline is hard, slow and resource-consuming because people are not driven by a customer-centric culture.
2   Business development: It is hard for organisations to use a service design approach to build better services because customer values are not always prominent. Service design remains something that is used only to create better customer experiences without optimising value to create a more profitable business.

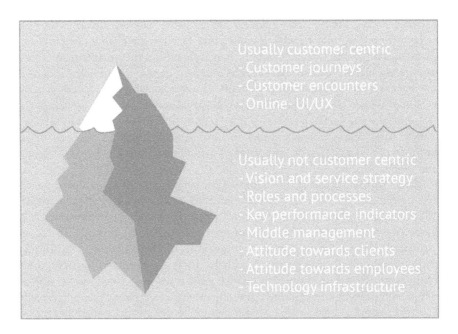

Figure 10.1 How customer-centric is your organisation?

Using the iceberg metaphor, our study reveals that customer-centricity is only the tip of the iceberg; most of the company culture lies under the water. In many organisations, customer-centric thinking does not reach below the waterline. People are still measured based on internal indicators; technological investments are not made based on customer value; and staff members' attitudes do not reflect customer value. To summarise, it is hard to create good output at the front end if the whole machine is not tuned to achieve that goal.

A colleague of mine, who is a social anthropologist, once said that customer-focused organisations have a modern totemic culture: everybody sees the same totem pole (of customer value); it drives all behaviours and attitudes and all decisions are made to achieve a common goal – how to create more value for our customers and thus become a better business.

When an organisation works in this way, change becomes easier. There is no need to justify or sell the idea for change; everybody knows what to do and why. However, for most organisations, especially large ones with deep silos, this does not come naturally. Wide and early participation in change processes can help. One good strategy is to get as many staff members as possible involved in the development process and to create a platform for change, preventing the submerged part of the iceberg from blocking the necessary changes. This sounds obvious, but it is rarely done, probably out of fear that involving staff members might lead to chaos, or prevent the organisation from performing daily tasks, or out of fear of change.

How can service design help organisations to change?

For humans, all change tends to feel strange, inauthentic or even unnatural at first. This is not a sign that the change does not work; it is a sign that we need to learn. For service designers who want to make changes, empathy is needed to understand these feelings, as well as to facilitate the process of learning. Organisational empathy is needed to understand why people want to stick to old models, why moving feels hard and what would motivate people to change.

New behaviours require the creation of many new habits. To establish new habits, cues are needed to trigger action and support the creation of routines, and people should feel rewarded for their investment of time and energy (Eyal 2014). Having organisational empathy allows service designers to understand possible mechanisms of habit creation. Sometimes it is a good strategy to try to infect a small cell within the company with a 'change virus'. When new habits start to become prevalent inside that cell, other cells might start to copy, steal or improve upon those new behaviours.

Two other important tools are participation and openness. As outsiders, service designers can be neutral and see the big picture. They can avoid taking sides in conflicts, and work as mediators and diplomats. However, they cannot do anything without help from the organisation. All cultural and behavioural changes need to start from the inside with people who are part of the machine. That puts a designer into the role of change facilitator, somebody who 'designs with and by people'. This role is discussed by Tim Brown in his book *Change by Design* (2009).

A change facilitators' goal is to turn the idea of change from a threat into an opportunity, and connect the internal forces that are needed to make the change happen. If you walk into somebody's room and tell them that they need to change, they will likely be belligerent and unwilling to listen. Fear of change is natural, but if you are able to find tools to help avoid it, you will save a lot of energy and resources. The best strategy is to start involving staff early, be open and honest and face the problems that must be dealt with as early as possible. Invite people to become co-designers of change. Services are all about people, and to change the core material of a service you need people to be involved. We call this involvement 'co-design of change'.

When changes are made in everyday routines, processes and leaderships, they affect the whole organisation and its internal dynamics. Involving people, especially people from different layers of the organisation, is always hard. This is a step that is often skipped because it is time-consuming and can feel superficial. At worst, it can stop change before it begins. Co-design that helps the change rather than complicating it needs to be facilitated carefully, and it often demands diplomacy, motivational training and psychology. For many designers, this is a new skillset, but it will help them become true facilitators of change.

The four principles for co-design of change

At Palmu, we faced obstacles from staff members when making changes in numerous projects. Based on those experiences, we developed a list of helpful practices that make involving staff easier. This list is not comprehensive, and you could easily make it longer with different practices, but we have looked at our successful change-making projects and picked these four principles that help the co-design of change. According to our experience, they are the small strategies with biggest impact – the habits of successful change facilitators.

All four principles are facilitator tools for service designers. With these tools, the designers are able to move the ownership of ideas to the people involved and help them to find their own motivation for change. This is crucial because when we talk about the lower part of the iceberg, we need to remember that organisational culture can never be changed from outside. Cultural change is something that only starts within the organisation, from people themselves as they realise motivations for new goals, receiving support from their managers and peers and spreading the messages. It is like a virus of new thoughts and behaviours, or a small revolution. At first, there needs to be talk. The talking then turns into doing, and eventually the doing can turn into new habits, routines and values if supported by knowledge, skills and desire (Covey 2004).

Yet, people's desire for and understanding of the good that the change may bring is at the core of talking turning into doing and the formation of new habits. Designing a process where people find this personal (and shared) desire is always tricky, but as with any other problem, some listening, friendly chat

Make people show and do their ideas
(instead of talking, explain with prototypes)

Let the owner take the stage
(when you explain to others, you start to believe)

Offer challenges
(build a path of small challenges
that leads towards finding the
right problem and solution)

More choices = more commitment
(choosing from options creates personal ownership)

Figure 10.2 Principles for co-design of change and everyday involvement.

and design empathy can help a lot. If the flame of desire is lit, it is rather easy to support that flame with new knowledge and skills that provide a basis for behavioural change. From the perspective of igniting the desire, there is also a difference in how you start your co-design of change. If people are invited to join, those who are ambitious see this as an opportunity and autonomously start setting themselves challenges and goals. If people are forced to join, you end up spending considerable energy attempting to create a setting that will create positive thinking. We have also learned that it is better not to expend much energy on those who are against everything. If you focus on the key influencers, who are easier to involve, in a positive 'way' and with a positive tone, they can become the ones to start the revolution from inside.

Co-design of change is really about developing the solutions together, making people feel meaningful and become the drivers of change themselves. However, it must be facilitated well or it will lead to chaos. We are still learning with every project and every new organisation culture; just like the minds of people, they are all different. These four principles are not magic, but they seem to build a bridge of openness between organisational silos and consultants who come from the outside.

Many organisations also have scars from the past that can prevent open involvement: previous bad experiences from change processes that cast their shadow upon everything new. If scars exist, they should not become taboos; rather, they need to be openly discussed. Instead of hiding difficult topics under the mattress and attempting to force the change, it is better to bring the issues into the open. Whatever is discussed in the coffee room after the workshop would be better discussed openly in the workshop.

Conclusion

There are two possible paths for the development of service design related to designing for change and change-making. From an industry perspective, it can either turn into a human-centric version of management consulting – an advisory tool for organisations to help them to determine how to offer more value to their customers – or it can become a toolbox for both finding the right direction and then executing the necessary change-making to build the right solution. The latter path is much harder, but also far more inspiring, because it takes us closer to actually having a measurable impact, both in the new behaviours inside the organisation and in the new behaviours of its customers.

Then, the next question is, if designers want to become change facilitators, what are the future skills that are needed? Working as a facilitator in a change process often feels more like being a therapist than a designer, and definitely requires excellent people skills. It also seems to be beneficial in conflict situations for a facilitator to not work permanently in the organisation. The ideal service designers are objective meditators who view the problems and needs in the social environment empathetically. They can help to contextualise problems so that they can be discussed as problems and not as people issues. They can also actively help the organisation to craft different solutions and experiment with those solutions as quickly as possible; that is, to become solution-centric rather than getting stuck in blaming the reasons for those problems. The power of being an outsider should not be underestimated. The practical second opinion and neutrality of a service designer as a therapist often trumps the organisational group therapy supported by self-help literature.

References

Brown, T. (2009) *Change by Design: How Design Thinking Transforms Organizations and Inspires Innovation.* New York: HarperCollins.
Covey, S.R. (2004) *The 7 Habits of Highly Effective People.* New York: Fireside.
Eyal, N. (2014) *Hooked: How to Build Habit-Forming Products.* New York: Penguin.
Merholz, P., Schauer, B., Verba, D. and Wilkens, T. (2008) *Subject to Change: Creating Great Products and Services for an Uncertain World.* Sebastopol, CA: O'Reilly Media.
Schein, E.H. (2004) *Organizational Culture and Leadership.* Hoboken, NJ: Jossey-Bass.

11 Introducing design thinking to large, technology-oriented companies

Marjukka Mäkelä

Keywords: ABB, user-centred design, user experience, business, customer, pilot

This chapter discusses how to transform a strongly tech-oriented R&D culture into a more agile and customer-oriented culture. The case example comes from ABB, which is a leading power and electronic company. With 140,000 employees and over 100 years of tech-driven history, it offers an interesting example of how to integrate user-centred design and design thinking into an R&D culture with a strong tradition of engineering. The chapter looks in more detail at the change agent pilot in the business unit of Drives and Controls.

In the face of new challenges

It is said that the rules in many industries are changing. Successful companies will no longer be the ones that make the best products, but the ones that gather the best data and combine it to offer the best digital services. Traditional methods of product and service development no longer suffice in the face of ever-increasing global competition. There is a need for a holistic approach, taking into account products, services and people – an approach like design thinking.

I operate in the business unit of Drives and Controls, which produces frequency converters. Over the past few decades, our business unit has grown larger, and with almost 7,000 people it has a salient internal role in ABB. In the past few years, we have been among the first units at ABB to establish a lean and agile product-development culture. Here, the themes of design thinking and user-centred design are a perfect match. Our business unit is divided into several independent profit units that take responsibility for their field of business in global R&D, sales and manufacturing. Collaboration between these profit units can be challenging as the scale of the units is considerable, and the organisational structure is silo-based.

Our R&D culture has been based firmly on an expert-driven design approach, where we rely on our design engineers' expertise and their assumptions on human behaviour. Our R&D culture embraces technical inventions and design engineering skills. We are excellent in terms of technology innovations. Today, however, technology as such has become a commodity.

Business dynamics are evolving, and digitalisation has led our customers to demand better experiences – not mere physical products. B2B follows B2C in the trend of service orientation. In our line of work, this means that technology and great product design must enable our future services. More holistic, seamless offerings will be taken for granted, and increased attention to consistent brand experience is required. This is exactly where design can make a difference.

Design in technology

I have a small team of designers in our business unit. We all have a background in industrial design, and the new competence we bring is in-house industrial design. By industrial design, I mean product design, service design and user interface (UI) design. These three design disciplines are commonly grounded in a user-centred design approach. Our work expands from tangible objects to services and digital solutions. Our ambition is to integrate user-centred design and design thinking into our R&D culture. We know it is not rocket science, but it is not a piece of cake either, especially in a large, tech-oriented company like ours.

Through our participation in several ongoing R&D projects, we designers experienced how the different teams struggled with the same topics concerning customer involvement, and saw how challenging it is to get customer insight into the projects. Moreover, we learned how much waste there can be if the organisation does not share its gained knowledge. In order to understand this challenge even better, we conducted a current-state analysis through semi-structured interviews with our product managers, sales and R&D engineers. We wanted to discover how people collect, store, share and utilise customer and user information across the organisation.

The findings were interesting. The sales people are on the frontline, meeting and talking with customers on an everyday basis, whereas R&D engineers are far away, receiving second-hand information about the customers and users. This information can often be filtered, biased and sometimes even lost completely on its way from the front to the back end. Perhaps years ago, when the organisation was much smaller, our design engineers were closer to the customers. They might have had hands-on experience using our equipment. Nowadays, there are many R&D persons that have never visited customer production sites, let alone met the end users. In order to improve this situation, we established a goal to balance the expert-driven approach with a user-centred design approach. This means introducing new strategies in our R&D to listen to, learn from and analyse customers and users. It means focusing on the latent needs of our users and determining systematic ways to co-create new solutions with them.

Design is about how well we can listen to and learn from different users and customers and turn these insights into usable knowledge. Design thinking means approaching a problem with a user-centred design mindset. The emphasis is on a holistic approach to design. That design focuses on more than the aesthetics of the physical products. It covers concerns related to human behaviour and needs throughout the whole development process, with the designers often being advocates for users within the R&D team. As Tim Brown (2009) puts it, in design thinking we combine what is *desirable* from a human point of view with what is *technologically feasible* and *economically viable*.

Organisations like ours are often unfamiliar with design thinking and design opportunities. Therefore, our work started with the design essentials; to make people understand that the main reason to involve professional industrial designers is to focus on how things feel, not on how they look. The meaningful functionality, ease of installation and operation of our equipment, as well as the efficient maintenance of our systems, are at the core of design activities.

CUX Ambassadors in practice

We initiated a pilot for the CUX Ambassadors programme. CUX comes from the words customer experience (CX) and user experience (UX). We wanted to try out a kind of change agent programme. I have heard that a good change agent has passion and aspiration for change, is open-minded and inspires others. Instead of trying to find this kind of participant, we actually examined the organisation chart and started to select people based on their managerial positions. Our pilot was about getting the key managers and senior experts on board first. Based on the interviews, we realised that there was no resistance but rather a lack of knowledge regarding user-centred design methods, and a lack of time to focus on customer and user needs. Thus, we needed middle management to buy in, in order to get them to encourage their peers and subordinates to carry out user-centred design activities. At the same time, we needed those managers to promote the concept to the top management.

New product development involves not only R&D design engineers and project managers but also other functions. From a customer-knowledge point of view, significant contributions were expected from our product-management and sales teams. This is why we ended up inviting 24 managers and senior experts from these three functions (R&D, product management, sales). They came from three different profit units. This created a unique forum for collaboration. Much effort was made to enable the participants to network and collaborate with each other. This became one of the core indicators of success of the pilot.

We asked the participants for three simple things: active participation in our six-month pilot; to take a leading position in cultural transformation; and to encourage others through their own actions. What we promised in return was to increase their understanding of future opportunities through user-centred design and design thinking, individual support on how to commit and implement change management within their own areas and, of course, a peer-to-peer way of working.

Our pilot consisted of a kick-off and five half-day workshops. Participants were divided into smaller teams that had their own tasks which facilitated the help of several meetings and learning diaries. During the pilot, we also utilised corporate social media tools (Yammer) to share interesting articles and videos, as well as to assign homework.

The programme had a significant element of training, and the implementation involved plenty of service-design methods. When we first met the future CUX Ambassadors, we introduced the current-state analysis results through playing cards. Gamification and visualisation played a key role in the programme. In the half-day workshops, we familiarised everyone with design methods and discussed how to integrate user-centred design into our R&D process, and how to become a design thinker. We watched video material from the field studies, training on observation skills and service-journey creation. We also utilised case examples and had a visitor from another company to share views and experiences regarding this same matter. One of the most valuable aspects of the whole pilot, based on participant feedback, was the diverse conversation and networking that occurred during the common sessions and team work.

Hands-on training and concrete examples of different methods were used to help participants transform their mindsets. We also utilised an activity measurement, created for this purpose, to follow up on participants' actions related to interactions with customers and internal networking and promotion. This provided visualisation of our achievements and made them more tangible.

In order to gain a deeper understanding of each participant's personal opinions and attitudes, we carried out in-depth interviews both at the beginning of the programme and at the end. One set of interviews was also conducted by external consultants, with whom we created and facilitated the whole pilot programme. The consultants interviewed members of the steering committee, who represented higher management (e.g. the head of R&D in the business unit).

My tips to be shared

I often quote Peter Drucker's famous phrase, 'Culture eats strategy for breakfast', as I feel strongly that even the best innovations can be lost if the company culture does not support the change. As the prevailing organisational structure can hinder (or support) the user-centred activities on a daily level, it is essential to understand the current culture and ways of working. My first tip is to *know your culture*; do some background research in order to understand your audience and users. If you wish to influence their mindset, the chances are better if you do this in a user-centred way. Conduct some contextual enquiries, observations and shadowing – perhaps even mystery shopping. I first started at ABB as an R&D project manager, then switched to working as a product manager. Those few years and positions prior to my current role as Manager for Industrial Design and UX were not the most obvious path for an industrial designer, yet those experiences taught me a lot about our company culture, our development process and truly enabled me to network.

Another tip is *never try to do it alone*; always get yourself a small circle of believers. Our small design team work like evangelists, repeating our message and trying to find yet another efficient way to illuminate others. Our CUX Ambassadors are another important group of design thinkers and promoters.

My final tip is to *be passionate yet patient*. Remember to take full advantage of your empathy skills along the way. Organisational inertia can be such a nuisance. Beyond the mere introduction of user-centred design methods, there is a need to ensure widespread adoption. This demands time, resources and effort. It also requires support from all managerial layers, with top management being the forerunner.

The recipe for success can be simple:

- Make sure that someone has ownership and responsibility to develop this topic.
- Make sure that you have a core team of professionals involved. Design competence does not grow by itself; it needs to be nurtured.
- Make sure the designers show the purpose of their work and integrate themselves into the rest of the organisation in an efficient yet smart way.
- Make sure your leaders are aware of the power of design thinking and user-centred design. If they are not yet, ensure that they will familiarise themselves with it quickly.

Conclusion

The CUX Ambassadors programme was set up to generate more awareness for user-centred design and design thinking. As a result, we have more people in our organisation who understand, promote and continue to work to become more customer-focused. Our task was, and still is, to convince our people that design can (and should) play an active role in the transformation of businesses. We need design competences in order to enable our organisation to shift our technology-oriented R&D process towards value co-creation, where projects are carried out by multidisciplinary teams specialising in technology, design and business.

We still face a great challenge in making our organisation see the value of design beyond simply enhancing product appearance. We are taking considerable steps towards balancing our traditional way of working with a user-centred design approach. The important message for everyone in our organisation is to understand that every individual can deliver and contribute to this topic in their everyday work. Rapid market changes in recent years have led to the introduction of companies that rely heavily on user-centred innovation to sustain their growth. Multidisciplinary teams are a certainty of the future.

We have worked along with and within the greater change programme inside ABB to introduce lean product development. The iterative and agile nature of design work, with a genuine interest in human behaviour and the voice of customers, is easy to include within lean product development. Design thinking enables us to identify what we should develop and deliver for our customers and users. At the same time, it suggests practical ways of working to be more productive and efficient. Knowing that you are doing the right things inevitably increases your motivation.

Transformation is not quick or painless, but what is great about user-centred design is that no one really argues against it. Every company would say that it is, or wants to be, customer-focused, but then you need to look at how they really do it. What is driving the change? Is it a genuine belief that through listening, interpreting and understanding customers they can succeed? This is an important question as it establishes the direction for internal transformation, as well as the key motivational message to employees. It also directs us towards the methods and tools for reshaping our culture. Internal collaboration, as well as co-creation with our customers, is the key to success.

Reference

Brown, T. (2009) *Change by Design: How Design Thinking Transforms Organizations and Inspires Innovation.* New York: HarperCollins.

12 How service design thinking empowers the evolution of corporate human resources

Arne van Oosterom, Michal Steckiw and Adolfo Martini

Keywords: Coca-Cola, employee experience, HR shared services, L'Oreal

Why do we work? What is our relationship to work, the company we work for and the people we work with? Why do we speak of a work–life balance as if these things are mutually exclusive? In this article, we will describe how our rapidly changing world is affecting people's relationships with work, and how service-design thinking can support HR professionals in playing a new and crucial role in supporting organisations in transformation.

Given the changing nature of the global workforce (rapidly growing percentage of millennials in the workforce), concerns regarding skill shortages and the gradual shift of 'power' to the employee, as well as changes in consumer behaviours related to new technologies, employee experience should be a primary focus area for any HR transformation programme, digital redesign projects for company portals and employee interaction tools, or when broadly creating a new HR strategy for any organisation. This is why some organisations are now using service design thinking to bring the 'H' back into HR.

Service design thinking is a human-centred approach to creating new, often innovative solutions to complex challenges impacting human experiences around products, services, environments and interactions. It is a method traditionally used by designers across various design disciplines, elevated by the technology industry and introduced successfully to the corporate world by companies such as Apple, Phillips and Google. The rapid evolution of digital technologies and their impact on consumer experiences have provided consumers with increasingly seamless interactions with every touchpoint with any brand, and have provided an opportunity for highly personalised and customised products and services. Even more, they have changed the traditional one-directional communication flow (brand to consumer), opening a real ongoing conversation (consumer to consumer to brand). Inspired and empowered by this shift in the consumer world, some forward-thinking companies are also applying the same customer-centric approach to their employee environments and employee services. These organisations are redesigning employee experiences using customer journey-mapping, prototyping and user-experience research, leveraging new user-centred, mobile-friendly and often cloud-based technologies.

Employee experience journey-mapping

As employees throughout our working lives, we all interact directly and indirectly with people (HR, managers, co-workers, customers) and systems (including processes, intranets and various technologies). Employee experience journey-mapping helps to capture, visualise or design these interactions. It is a methodology based upon the highly successful Customer Experience Journey-Mapping tool. It can be used to better understand specific employee journeys, uncovering pain points and opportunity areas that can lead to improvements and innovations to create better employee experiences across physical and digital interactions – experiences that reflect a company's identity and culture.

Based upon this mapping exercise, companies identify moments of truth, moments that matter the most to the employees, developing future service scenarios aimed to redesign and improve the employee experience. This influences the attitudes that will ultimately drive the outcomes companies desire, whether it is a hiring and on-boarding process, employee engagement or employee separation and off-boarding. With an understanding of employee journeys, organisations are able to take a holistic design approach that results in new experiences that deliver desired outcomes, both for employees and the company.

Employee experience journey-mapping is all about looking at how HR services can be experienced from the perspective of an employee – the end user of any HR service. The goal is to achieve both defined business objectives and reinforce the sense of belonging to an organisation.

Employee experience

Employee experience is more than just having a nice user experience in the HR system or a company portal. There are different aspects of employee experience. Any journey usually begins long before the departure. It involves many actors, each responsible for a part of a journey. How and what employees experience depends on the communication strategy and its execution, the employer branding strategy, the HR service process and technology (SAP, Workday), high touch support and the way in which employees are engaged. This is where employee experience journey-mapping helps to understand how HR services are delivered from the perspective of an employee, with the goal of achieving defined business objectives and meeting employee needs in a simplified, intuitive, easy-to-follow and, whenever possible, enjoyable way.

Today, employees, just like consumers, are seeking a sense of purpose in their day-to-day jobs and a personal alignment with the company's values, way of working, opportunities for growth and acquisition of all the skills required to fulfil the position. In this scenario, interactions with digital technologies and complex systems have to be intuitive, considerate and designed around their needs. Through observations and behaviour analysis, companies can draw conclusions about what employees want and need in order to build empathy with end users and meet those needs. In the end, the role of HR is to support, develop and often enable employees to meet their daily job and strategic role objectives. Very often, conclusions from empathic or user-experience research are hard to express in quantitative language. Instead, service design uses emotional language concerning aspirations, desires, engagement, experience and challenges. The work to understand employees – the end users – is deeper and more ethnographic than quantitative and statistical. Project teams may discuss the emotional resonance of a value proposition as much as they would discuss utility, process and technology requirements.

A number of companies are already redesigning their HR functions in that direction, including well-known global brands such as Cisco, Coca-Cola and L'Oreal. A move to consumerised employee experiences helps companies to create a more enjoyable and effective work environment, attract the best talent and put the 'human' back into human resources.

The Coca-Cola Company

By 2030, millennials (those born somewhere between 1980 and the early 2000s) are expected to account for 75% of the global workforce. As a generation, they bring with them consumer expectations shaped by the experience of online services from the likes of Google and Apple – and they expect the same quality of digital services in the workplace. These expectations are a major challenge for businesses worldwide, requiring firms to innovate in the way they hire, manage and grow the best talent. For Coca-Cola, service design has allowed the company to achieve a structured understanding of how to ensure a desirable HR experience. This has helped its Global Business Services division (GBS) to redesign HR services based on customer journey maps, prototypes and service blueprints. This required acquiring and developing a service design thinking capability. Working with the HR team and employees from across the company resulted in gathering essential insights and drawing a customer journey map for Coca-Cola GBS HR services. The result is a complete service experience that is intuitive and enjoyable and incorporates mobile and digital technologies, including new end-to-end customer-centric GBS HR services based on user insights and journey-mapping, and new digital, mobile-friendly, user-centric communication tools for embedding Coca-Cola's consumer brand values of happiness, togetherness, engagement and inspiration into the employee experience. The impact of these projects is clear – when services are organised around employees' needs, we have seen a significant increase in employee engagement, satisfaction and productivity.

L'Oreal

L'Oreal is the world leader in beauty, present in 130 countries on five continents. Compared to other industries, the cosmetic business is extremely dynamic and sophisticated. To win the race, you need people who are passionate, have a strong entrepreneurial spirit, are able to understand customers and quickly turn insights into relevant innovations. Engagement and talent retention is therefore a key success factor to ensure a competitive advantage: the rare ability to deal with intangible concepts, aspirations and human needs while, at the same time, being excellent in terms of operational execution.

When the talent war started in the early 2000s, L'Oreal's HR team suddenly realised that securing the talent pipeline had become a top priority. They decided to focus on the critical phase of the employee experience journey: the first two years within the group. The challenge was how to drastically reduce the turnover of newcomers and facilitate their inclusion into the company culture and way of working.

L'Oreal developed a human-centred concept called 'FIT' (Follow-up and Integration Track), with the clear intention to empathise with new employees at L'Oreal, regardless of the country, function or level of their job. FIT is a bilateral condition (person and organisation), not a rigid model to which everyone must adapt. It is customised around every single new employee, yet based on a common and solid framework.

Service design for HR

Using this consumer-centred approach – putting HR into the new employee's shoes – the company was able to provide solutions at the global level (induction plan, field assignments, on-the-job learning activities, connections with a mentor, key company culture-related trainings, exposure to senior executives, etc.) that could be adapted and contextualised to the specific reality in every country.

Cisco also redesigned its HR services around employee needs. To the delight of its employees, the company identified 'moments that matter'; that is, needs or events that employees view as particularly important. Moments that matter vary across organisations and constitute life or work events that have the greatest impact on employee satisfaction, productivity and business results. Cisco determined that such moments included joining the organisation, changing jobs or geographies and managing family emergencies. The company redesigned its employee services around these moments.

Conclusion

Service design thinking can help to understand and redesign each aspect of employee experience, leveraging new technologies and responding to the changing aspirations and needs of tomorrow's workforce – starting from recruitment and new employee integration, and moving through learning and development, the everyday work environment, collaboration and reporting, and so on. Companies embark on that design journey with various projects: re-shaping career websites, employee communication design, intranet redesign, recruitment and assessment processes, employee integration and engagement and workspace environments.

Employees, as consumers, expect the same kind of delightful, seamless and often personalised digital experiences they enjoy in their everyday consumer lives. Although design thinking is not specifically referred to as such, there is one shared objective: redesigning the employee experience through digital and physical fusion and changing organisations by design rather than only by process optimisation.

Part IV

Tools for industrial service design

Service design tools for industry

13 A heuristic to increase the innovativeness potential of groups

Maurício Manhães

Keywords: heuristic, innovation, groups

Service design has enabled organisations to design and deliver innovative service propositions. Nevertheless, to fulfil its potential, service design demands a certain level of collaboration among diverse groups of people, both from inside and outside the organisation. While this required diversity presents possibilities for innovativeness, it strengthens the need for intergroup interaction and communication and 'might lead to conflict and distrust' (Østergaard et al. 2011). In this chapter, innovativeness is defined as a measure of the degree of 'newness' that is perceived by a social group with regard to a specific product. To face the challenge of creating innovative propositions, it is first necessary to overcome the hurdles of diversity. Based on decades of research about human intergroup contact, a heuristic is proposed to support managers in facing the triple challenge of innovativeness.

The triple challenge of innovativeness

According to the theories on how humans understand and interpret expressions from each other, to innovate, individuals must overcome the triple challenge of: (1) a flickering self-awareness; (2) understanding what is the 'other' (Gadamer 2004); to finally (3) 'create anything new of importance' (Schumpeter 1912) – that is, to create innovative propositions. Demanding all of this of any single person would seem to be too much, regardless of what toolkit is provided.

What is supposed to happen when someone is faced with this triple challenge of innovativeness is that new knowledge should be created. To create innovative propositions, it is expected that people adopt and apply specific heuristics to find creative pathways to solve problems or overcome obstacles that seemed impossible, based on previous perspectives and knowledge. In all cases, these challenges can only be overcome by creating new knowledge and discovering new ways of augmenting the potential to act (Von Krogh 2013: 4). Such knowledge, in turn, can only be created by building bridges between the different, as arcs, *herméneutiques* (Ricœur 1986: 158), connecting seemingly incompatible concepts.

In addition to the concept of the individual triple challenge, to reap the highest benefits from employing service-design toolkits to improve innovation, organisations also have to overcome the correspondent triple challenge of: (1) understanding the prejudices of their members; (2) understanding the historical context and, finally; (3) creating meaningful and innovative propositions.

Organisations can facilitate this process by providing their members with a heuristic to support the sense-making (Weick 1995) process inherent to the challenges of generating service innovativeness proposals.

Heuristic based on innovativeness determinants related to prejudice

The possibility of being aware of one's own closed-mindedness, which is 'of key importance to the ways in which our thoughts, often inchoate and unwieldy, congeal to form clear-cut subjective knowledge' (Kruglanski 2004), has elicited a fair amount of discussion, particularly after the Second World War (Allport 1979). Nevertheless, it remains a controversial subject. One of the most academically accepted (or least criticised) ways of reducing ignorance about the negative impacts of a person's own closed-mindedness is through group dynamics, which foster 'cooperative learning' under positive conditions of equal status, shared goals, cooperation and sanction by authority (Paluck and Green 2009: 345).

Based on studies and data generated by decades of research about intergroup contact and closed-mindedness (Allport 1979; Kruglanski 2004; Manhães 2015; Pettigrew 1998; Roets and Van Hiel 2011), it is possible to support the challenges of generating service innovativeness proposals with quantitative and qualitative arguments.

The sense-making discourse that supports this heuristic is structured as follows, based on twelve determinants:

1 When people feel confident in a group, they will want it to be long-lived.
2 To have longevity, a group needs to have good performance.
3 To have good performance, a group needs to innovate.
4 To innovate, a group must go through *Bildung* processes.
5 To go through a *Bildung* process, a group needs the benefits of sociocultural diversity.
6 To have the benefits of sociocultural diversity, a group has to be aware of the prejudices of its members.
7 To be aware of the prejudices of its members, a group needs to obtain evidence.
8 To obtain evidence, a group has to be committed to act.
9 To commit to act, a group has to be enabled to act.
10 To be enabled to act, a group has to create new knowledge.
11 To create new knowledge, a group's members need to feel confident.
12 Feeling confident in a group, the group members will want group activity to be long-lived.

At this point, it is necessary to make two essential clarifications. The first is about the word *Bildung*. The second is to explain why the longevity determinant is at the beginning and end of the heuristic. In English, the German word *Bildung* corresponds to 'formation' and can be described as 'keeping oneself open to what is other – to other, more universal points of view' (Gadamer 2004), which can be considered a fundamental condition for co-creation efforts, especially with regard to obtaining innovative propositions.

To understand why longevity appears twice in the heuristic, it is necessary to be aware that, from a sense-making perspective, organisations are collectives, whose participants have a common interest in the organisations' longevity (Scott 1987; Weick 1995). Therefore, to act into the future to enhance the longevity of a group from an interesting perspective, research indicates that efforts should be invested in reducing conflicts with stakeholders as a way to boost confidence in a group or organisation. Whereas the first longevity determinant is focused on the future, the second is aimed at checking the past. It is a point of reflection; a historical point where the group retrospectively evaluates its past efforts to build confidence, generate evidence and foster innovativeness. After all, the interest in the longevity of a group arises in retrospect as a result of plausible explanations about what is occurring to the individuals inside a particular group or organisation.

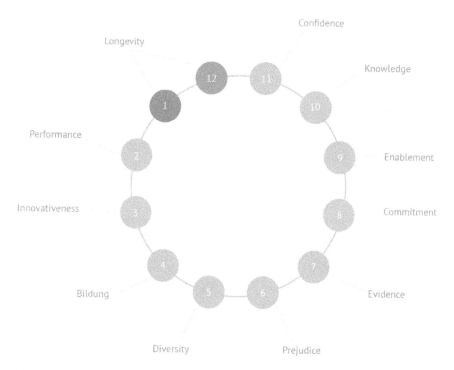

Figure 13.1 Heuristic based on innovativeness determinants related to prejudice.

At the same time, this heuristic works to avoid both contradictory perspectives of: (1) the constraints of a 'method' for service innovation; and (2) proposing 'tyrannies of structurelessness' (Alvesson and Sköldberg 2009: 160). This 'middle way' takes into account the hermeneutic experience and invites those involved to play with their understandings that are at stake. And, as a sense-making discourse, play is precisely what innovation is: there is a risk that it 'will not "work," "succeed," or "succeed again," which is the attraction of the game' (Gadamer 2004: 106).

The main goal of the heuristic is to enable people to act by promoting the necessary mindset to use service-design toolkits. Therefore, this heuristic serves to support the execution of ad-hoc innovativeness projects. During the development of a new product (goods or service), organisations can use the determinants of this heuristic to support decision-making for the upcoming steps of the project. In a sense, its determinants ensure that project leaders are aware of the hermeneutic conditions necessary to apply service-design toolkits to innovative purposes.

Innovativeness potential check

Based on the proposed heuristic, it is possible to suggest an innovativeness potential check for organisations. This check is designed to be used by managers in order to verify whether the respective innovativeness group has the highest potential to face the triple challenge of innovativeness.

The proposed check process is based on four questions, which managers must answer with 'Yes' or 'No'. The questions are:

- Are organisational members, as a whole, or the group directly responsible for the innovative effort composed of a balanced mix of different-minded (open and closed) individuals?
- Does this group obey a governance policy that enforces intergroup contact conditions: equal status, common goals and interdependence?
- Does this group have complete autonomy to define courses of action, milestones, goals and deliverables?
- Was the group clearly informed about the resources (budget and time frame) with which it is obliged to comply?

These questions are directly related to the proposed heuristic. To augment the probability of overcoming the triple challenge of innovativeness, based on the reasoning that supports the present heuristic, organisational managers have to respond positively (Yes) to all questions presented above. Each negative answer prompts managers to implement actions and directives to deal with each of the aspects related to these questions.

Conclusion

The proposed heuristic, based on decades of research, was developed and applied by research studies in workshops in five different countries, with more than 180 people of 10 different nationalities. The results of these studies indicate that the adoption of the proposed heuristic by groups is a positive and significant predictor of their potential to create products that will be perceived as innovative by independent judges (Manhães 2015).

In fact, groups that adopted this heuristic had their products perceived as more innovative by independent judges (*ibid*). The same phenomenon can be seen when assessing particularly innovative groups, such as start-up organisations. Any organisational groups where the mindset mix is focused both on possibilities and restraints (Q1 and Q4), on horizontal hierarchies that promote interdependence and common goals (Q2), and on speed and disregard for the status-quo that drive autonomy (Q3) are working under the proposed heuristic.

References

Allport, G. (1979) *The Nature of Prejudice*, 25th Anniversary edition. New York: Perseus Books.

Alvesson, M. and Sköldberg, K. (2009) *Reflexive Methodology: New Vistas for Qualitative Research*. Thousand Oaks, CA: Sage.

Gadamer, H-G. (2004) *Truth and Method*, 2nd edition, London: Continuum.

Kruglanski, A.W. (2004) *The Psychology of Closed Mindedness (Essays in Social Psychology)*. New York: Psychology Press.

Manhães, M.C. (2015) *Innovativeness and Prejudice: Designing a Landscape of Diversity for Knowledge Creation*. Florionópolis: Universidade Federal de Santa Catarina, Centro Tecnológico.

Østergaard, C.R., Timmermans, B. and Kristinsson, K. (2011) Does a different view create something new? The effect of employee diversity on innovation. *Research Policy*, 40(3), pp. 500–509.

Paluck, E.L. and Green, D.P. (2009) Prejudice reduction: What works? A review and assessment of research and practice. *Annual Review of Psychology*, 60, pp. 339–367.

Pettigrew, T.F. (1998) Intergroup contact theory. *Annual Review of Psychology*, 49(1), pp. 65–85.

Ricœur, P. (1986) *Du texte à l'action, Essais d'herméneutique II*. Paris. Éditions du Seuil.

Roets, A. and Van Hiel, A. (2011) Item selection and validation of a brief, 15-item version of the Need for Closure Scale. *Personality and Individual Differences*, 50(1), pp. 90–94.

Schumpeter, J.A. (1912) *The Theory of Economic Development: The Economy as a Whole*. Leipzig: Duncker & Humblot.

Scott, W.R. (1987) *Organizations: Rational, Natural, and Open Systems*, 2nd edition. Englewood Cliffs, NJ: Prentice Hall.

Von Krogh, G. (2013) *Towards Organizational Knowledge: The Pioneering Work of Ikujiro Nonaka*. Basingstoke & New York: Palgrave Macmillan.

Weick, K.E. (1995) *Sensemaking in Organizations*. London: Sage.

14 What happens before service design?

Paula Bello

Keywords: Kone Corporation, Creagent, Guidio, Meeting Assistant, strategy, case study, start-up, family business, corporation

Every company has its own DNA, its own history and its own path. Providing a recipe for implementing service design simply does not work. Whether you are building or restoring a house, creating a health plan or building a government policy, it is wise to start with an analysis of the strengths, weaknesses, opportunities and threats you face. The same applies when considering applying service design in any industry.

There is plenty of literature that outlines methods and tools for implementing service design thinking. However, there is not much to help you understand yourself before deciding to use service design. Having a realistic understanding of where you are and where you want to go will help you create a plan in which service design can meet your specific needs.

This chapter presents an analysis model to help you evaluate how service design can best serve you before you begin implementing it. The model considers two key steps: diagnosis and action.

The analysis model summarises the lessons learned from very different companies that share many experiences, challenges and opportunities:

1 Kone: A B2B global corporation founded in 1910, with almost 50,000 employees and sales of over €8.6 billion.
2 BEDAR Group: A 110-year-old family business providing hospitality and property services that is in generational transition.
3 Creagent, Guidio and Meeting Assistant: Three start-ups that have been operating for less than three years and have fewer than ten employees.

Why service design?

Since I started to apply service design in a variety of industries, I have become a very strong advocate of its power. It is the most efficient approach for any business to achieve user- and customer-centricity (Bello 2015). Furthermore, it is a highly scalable practice that yields positive results regardless of the size and conditions of the project. All the chapters in this book showcase examples of those benefits. However, I have learned that you need a strong, solid foundation upon which to work; one cannot start at the same place or copy models from different projects. In a way, a company is like a house, and service design like a refurbishment project. To create changes that are beneficial and sustainable, you must start by fixing the foundation and infrastructure.

So, what is service design? There are several definitions that lead us towards a common understanding. For many years, the Service Design Network, (SDN) used to define it on their website as:

> the activity of planning and organizing people, infrastructure, communication and material components of a service in order to improve its quality and the interaction between service provider and customers. The purpose of service-design methodologies is to design according to the needs of customers or participants, so that the service is user-friendly, competitive and relevant to the customers.

One of my favourite explanations of service design was given in a conversation between the founder of SDN, Birgit Mager, and a pioneering service designer, Oliver King. For Mager,

> service design as a discipline provides an organisation with a proven set of tools and methodologies that span two gaps: what customers want and what an organisation can provide, and the look and feel of a service; how to orchestrate systems, processes, and resources to produce the desired result.

And for King, 'Service Design is a collaborative process of researching, envisaging, and then orchestrating experiences that happen over time and multiple touch points' (Mager and King 2009).

All definitions include the involvement of the individuals that will eventually buy and use the product or service. Thus, users focus on what is really important for them. This is called customer- and user-centricity. In that sense, this discipline is not new. For instance, the now widely recognised maternity package from the Finnish Social Security Institution (KELA),[1] commonly known as the 'Finnish baby box', is a kit given to all expectant or adopting parents who live in Finland, or who are covered by the Finnish social security system. The package contains children's clothes and other necessary items, such as nappies, bedding, a towel, muslin cloths and other child-care products, but its purpose and impact goes beyond the products themselves.

In the 1920s, General Carl Mannerheim realised that malnutrition was not only a constant among army personnel but also one of the main causes of the Finnish Civil War in 1918. Between 1937–1949, his sister, nurse Sophie Mannerheim, founder of *Mannerheimin Lastensuojeluliitto* (the Mannerheim Child Welfare Association), together with doctor Arvo Ylppö, developed a concept to provide poor mothers with loaned baby clothes and other necessities. The concept developed in the following years, giving birth to *Neuvola* (Child Health Centre), and since 1949, the 'box' has been given to all mothers who visit their local Child Health Centres. The contents and their design continue to evolve to match contemporary needs (e.g. disposable nappies were substituted for reusable ones in 2000), practices (e.g. children can sleep in the box to reduce the chance of suffocation) and fashion (there are yearly competitions for gender-neutral item designs).

The implications of this user-centred product–service combination cannot be minimised. From a health perspective, child mortality was reduced from 95 to 2.9 deaths per 1,000 children between 1936 and 2011. From the mother's perspective, receiving the box is a key moment in pregnancy; many have described it as a bonding and internalising moment for the family and new child. From the child's perspective, it provides the same start in life for all Finnish newborns, regardless of the social, economic, political or religious standing of the parents.

This is just one historical example of a great solution for a greater challenge. What is new is the professionalisation of the practices, tools, methods and processes used to systematise the conceptualisation of that sort of problem and its solution. This is what we call the design-thinking approach.

Why start before service design?

The reason for building service design capabilities is to ensure that users and customers are at the core of the organisation and its solutions. To define what that goal is, one needs a purpose, which was the first critical factor identified in the analysed industries. To define a purpose, one needs clarity of one's vision and mission, but often, we do not understand what each term means. A *vision* is the optimal desired future. It is focused and clear enough to be understood by employees, customers and users, and it inspires people to achieve it. A *mission* defines why an organisation exists and how it is going to reach that vision, including what it does, for whom it does it and how it does it.

Furthermore, when one takes part in a service design project, one can expect that the results will require incremental to drastic changes in processes within the organisation. New processes involve people changing their behaviour, and changing behaviour requires the right attitude. Therefore, the other critical factor is the right attitude towards change and a user- and customer-centred service.

A clear purpose for the industry and a positive attitude within the organisation are the two most fundamental elements of a strong foundation for a user- and customer-centred organisation. Both are needed across a company, from top management to the operative level. If we are to create the best possible products and services for our customers and end users, we must start by understanding ourselves and our staff, customers and users.

Step 1: diagnosis

Asking the right questions is fundamental to understanding where you are. You should ask rather simple questions to ensure that everyone can understand. From this, a more critical analysis of why you are where you are can be performed.

The following matrix synthesises an approach that has been proven to be very effective in all industries, regardless of size or complexity. Mark where you find your organisation on both axes and define the quadrant in which you are situated.

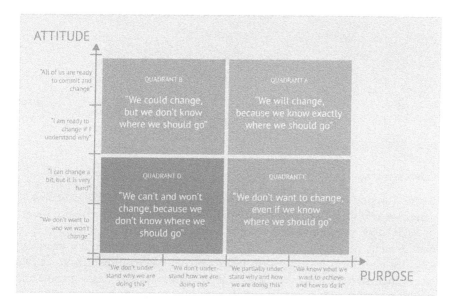

Figure 14.1 Diagnosis matrix.

Step 2: action plan

Organisations rarely score 100% in terms of purpose and attitude. Nonetheless, by defining where you are, you can start defining a plan and roadmap for where to go. Service design can support your organisation at different levels and in different ways by using different practices, methodologies and tools.

The following matrix can help you find your way and describes some of the most common tools that can help you perform specific tasks.

You seldom have the luxury of taking one step at a time, especially if you are located in the critical area of Quadrant D. However, if you do not have a clear vision and an actionable mission, it will be very difficult to engage your team. If you engage your team from the beginning to define your vision and mission, the entire process will be made easier.

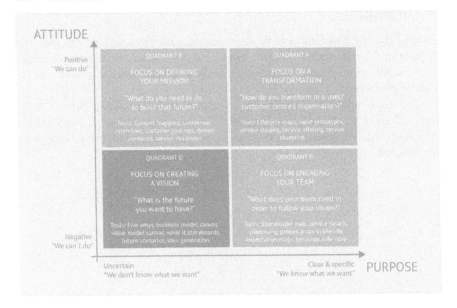

Figure 14.2 Action plan matrix.

Case studies

Kone Corporation has the right momentum to start to implement service design. A few years ago, the vision, mission and values of the company were updated and communicated very clearly across the organisation. Top management decided to transform the culture from 'engineering products' towards 'customer- and user-driven solutions'. That required actions at two levels: their strategic targets needed to be transformed into clear, tangible and actionable value propositions; and they needed a combination of life-cycle services and products in a holistic solutions portfolio.

Most parts of the organisation are committed to making necessary changes, and there has been a dynamic process of reorganisation of resources. However, owing to the company's size, the resources needed to implement significant changes are massive and decision-making processes are slow. We can still position this corporation in Quadrant A since it has a clear purpose and attitude, even if achieving its objective will be challenging.

In this case, service design can be used at any level of the organisation, from strategic-level planning to small pilots to further engage employees, and even customers and users. Because of the size of the company, a holistic, long-term plan with a good set of resources is needed to have a visible impact. In my experience, the best way to start planning is by *doing;* small pilot projects make a huge difference. On one hand, they require minor investment; on the other hand, they allow the company to investigate what service design can mean to the organisation and offer tangible proof of its benefits. After obtaining the results from the first pilots, the discussion moves from a theoretical approach towards a concrete and tangible proposal. Showing actual results instead of lecturing on the potential results provides a much stronger discourse.

The BEDAR Group family business is undergoing a generational transition, and operates within the property and hospitality industries. The growth has been mostly organic and fragmented, and characterised by periods of prosperity and crisis. It is pretty much a textbook example of a family business directed by a single family member. However, the new generation has decided to create a professional board and institutionalise the operations. The board is now at the phase of redefining the company's vision and mission, while modernising and focusing operations and business models.

The biggest challenge is the organisation's strong resistance to change owing to long-established paternalistic practices, both at the ownership and operational levels. Although changes usually occur very slowly, the board is faced with making drastic organisational transformations. Therefore, communication and engagement inside and outside the organisation are needed. Thus, we can place this enterprise in Quadrant C.

In this case, service design is most beneficial to test the vision and mission statement, and engage employees so they can participate in the redefinition of the vision and mission and feel like they are participating in the change. It can also be used to define customers' journeys regarding the services provided, to differentiate them from the organisation's historical practices ('a renewed service') and competing organisations. If employees cannot change their behaviour, they may be required to leave the organisation. This may make shifting to a customer- and user-centric organisation a painful process.

Creagent, Guidio and Meeting Assistant are three start-ups that were all born out of the needs and opportunities of our time. A user-centric approach is already embedded in their operating practices. Their attitudes are user-centric and characterised by high motivation and commitment among their founders and employees. However, they differ in the clarity of their purposes. As a result of to their small size, changes can be implemented rather quickly. However, they are affected by the strong competition they have for funding. In a way, some of their first customers were investors, and investors focus not only on value propositions or solutions but also on the company's potential to return on their investments. Therefore, the key challenge is determining how to build the desired future, both at the solution and resource levels. The three companies are positioned in Quadrants B and D.

The companies in Quadrant D must define their visions. Often, when an individual starts a company with a great idea, they need to be self-critical and move further away from it to obtain a long-term perspective, and identify what they really want to achieve. Usually, there are many paths to follow to achieve goals. As each company has several desired futures, scenarios are a good way to evaluate options and validate them with key actors.

The companies located in Quadrant B have efficient user and customer journeys, a clear mission and roadmaps to allow resources to be allocated to the aspects of the service experience that can yield the biggest impact with the smallest amount of resources.

Of the three cases, the start-ups offered the most possibility for service design owing to their agility and attitudes. The key to benefitting from service design here is to identify opportunities and weaknesses very precisely and only focus on developing those. The start-ups must overcome the speed of business and fierce competition, so it is essential to have an extremely focused purpose and an assertive attitude. They need to translate their vision and mission into products and services, with targeted and differentiated value propositions that enchant and engage investors, customers and users. If that happens, success will follow.

Conclusion

The chapters in this book present many ways in which service design can make a difference to your organisation. The number of successful cases will increase as the field gains greater experience and relevance. Service design has a high degree of scalability, so you can start by taking small steps and determine how it could be implemented in your organisation.

I recommend looking critically at your organisation, mainly in terms of the two key factors of success for a service design project: purpose and attitude. If you have both, you are on a path to accomplishing your goals. Service design can help you to take further steps towards customer- and user-centric solutions and practices, as well as clarify your vision and mission, engage your team and bring you closer to your customers and end users.

Note

1   www.kela.fi/web/en/maternitypackage.

References

Bello, P. (2015) So what did you say service design is? *Touchpoint: The Journal of Service Design*, 7(2). pp. 56–61.

Mager, B. and King, O. (2009) Methods and processes of service design. *Touchpoint: The Journal of Service Design*, 1(1), pp. 20–29.

15 Designing a service-dominant business model in the industrial context

Katri Ojasalo

Keywords: service-dominant logic, business model, industry, value, canvas

This chapter introduces a comprehensive, easy-to-use tool for use in designing a customer-centred business model in the industrial context. This tool can help industrial companies implement their service-dominant strategies and facilitate value creation for their customers. When used in a service design process, this business model tool helps industrial companies better utilise the insight of their business customers, and design integrated solutions that correspond with their customers' future needs.

Why are service-dominant business tools needed in the industrial context?

Many industrial companies desire to improve their profit margins. At the same time, their customers are increasingly demanding turnkey solutions instead of products that only partially solve their problems. Consequently, industrial companies have begun to design integrated solutions to solve their customers' problems in an attempt to differentiate themselves from their competitors and create competitive advantage. The use of this kind of logic when focusing on industrial service growth is compelling: engaging in new business with current customers tends to create greater customer loyalty, new unique selling points, higher margins and faster innovation.

However, adopting the role of a service provider is often demanding because an industrial service business model requires a very different approach from a pure manufacturing business model. While a pure manufacturing business model concentrates on selling products, a service approach focuses on facilitating value creation for customers and co-creating value with them. Customers may not value the proposed service models if they cannot see clear added value compared to the current form of cooperation. Thus, industrial service providers require a wide range of competencies to handle both the product and the service aspects of their offerings (Ojasalo 2007).

When industrial companies become facilitators and value co-creators, they engage deeply with their customers' processes. Adopting this kind of service-dominant business logic means that an industrial company must constantly search for possibilities to understand and support their customers' value creation processes (e.g., Grönroos and Ravald 2011). Consequently, a more holistic understanding of the customer's business, processes, practices and experiences is needed. This requires companies to build their businesses based on in-depth insights into customers' activities and context and to analyse what implications these have for their business (see Heinonen et al. 2010).

However, most companies still operate in terms of traditional industrial logic, which focuses on the supplier company's process. The reason for this may not always be ignorance of the emerging service-dominant business thinking. In fact, managers and developers still have too few tools with which to implement customer-centred, service-dominant strategies (Ojasalo and Ojasalo 2015). Popular business tools that direct companies' planning and decisions are based mostly on traditional industrial logic: 'We are selling something *to* someone'. There is a clear need for tools that truly help industrial companies develop their business models with their customers' everyday processes and problems in mind: 'How can we create new value together *with* our customers?'

Service Logic Business Model Canvas covers both value capture and value creation

The Service Logic Business Model Canvas (Ojasalo and Ojasalo 2015) responds to the above need by covering both the industrial company's viewpoint (value capture) and its customer's viewpoint (value creation). This tool forces industrial service designers to systematically consider the customer's viewpoint and their everyday business and processes, with respect to each element of the business model. The testing of this tool in several companies has shown that the Service Logic Business Model Canvas is a relevant and easy-to-use tool that can help companies implement customer-centred strategies, focusing on customer value creation. The development process of the canvas lasted over 18 months, and more than 100 persons and 70 companies were involved in the process (Ojasalo and Ojasalo 2015).

Like the original Business Model Canvas (Osterwalder and Pigneur 2010), the Service Logic Business Model Canvas is composed of nine building blocks (see Figure 15.1). In each block of the canvas, both the industrial service provider viewpoint ('from our point of view') and the customer viewpoint ('from a customer's point of view') are considered. The customer viewpoint forces industrial service designers to analyse their business and offerings from the perspective of their customers' goals, practices and experiences. Thus, designing a service-dominant business model also needs to be more customer-centred, and various service-design (and foresight) methods should be used for information gathering, ideation and development work (see Ojasalo et al. 2015). In other words, the effective application of the Service Logic Business Model Canvas requires a large amount of customer information, which can be generated with the help of various service-design methods before beginning to fill in the canvas.

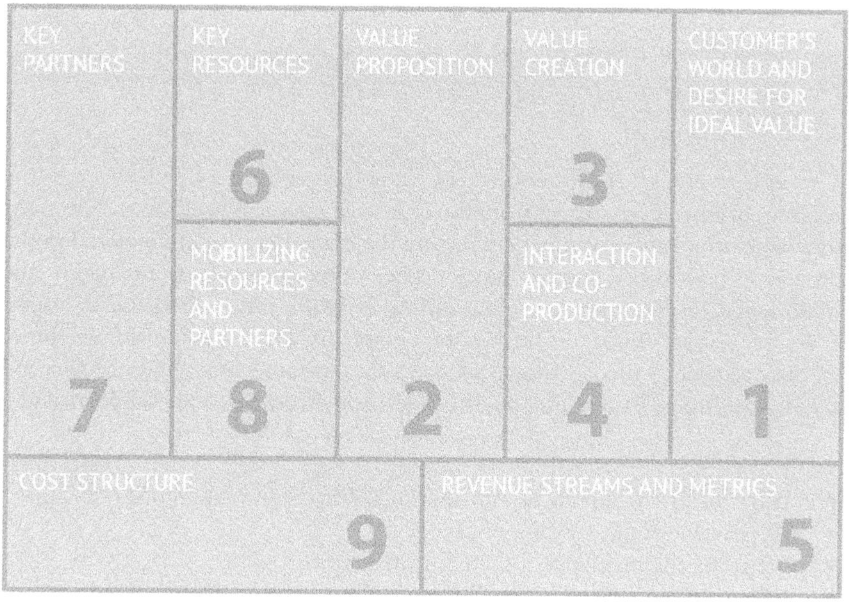

KEY PARTNERS	KEY RESOURCES	VALUE PROPOSITION	VALUE CREATION	CUSTOMER'S WORLD AND DESIRE FOR IDEAL VALUE
	6		3	
	MOBILIZING RESOURCES AND PARTNERS		INTERACTION AND CO-PRODUCTION	
7	8	2	4	1
COST STRUCTURE			REVENUE STREAMS AND METRICS	
	9			5

Figure 15.1 Service Logic Business Model Canvas.
Source: Based on Ojasalo and Ojasalo, 2015: 321.

The canvas is then best filled in in a co-design workshop, where the customer data is processed together with various stakeholders. The contents of the Service Logic Business Model Canvas are shown briefly in Figure 15.1.

1. Customer's world and desire for ideal value

The first block (1) to be filled in during a co-design session is called 'customer's world and desire for ideal value'. In other words, before moving to the value proposition and other blocks of a business model, it is essential to discuss in depth the customer's (and the customer's customer's) business to obtain a holistic understanding of the customer's world: context, activities, practices, experiences etc. In this block, the customer's explicit and latent problems and motivations, as well as the goals and benefits that the customer desires, are analysed. In addition to functional and economic benefits, customers may also value emotional, social, ethical, environmental and symbolic factors. The information in this block is often based on the customer personas created during a service-design process. The personas illustrate typical customer profiles, and are often based on the data generated during interviews, observations, probes, workshops etc. The questions to be answered in the first block include the following:

- How do we obtain a deep insight and holistic understanding of the customers' worlds, their future strategies and their own customers' world?
- Why do the customers buy?

- What kind of benefits (functional, economic, emotional, social, ethical, environmental, or symbolic) do the customers desire?

2. Value proposition

The second block (2) of the canvas is 'value proposition', which specifies the impact customers can expect from the industrial company's offering. Naturally, the value proposition should be based on the customer insight described in the previous 'customer's world' block. The value proposition highlights the importance of capturing what the customer really buys when the industrial company sells its solution. The industrial company's offering should correspond to the customer's mental model of what the customer intends to obtain and achieve via the offering. The questions to be answered include the following:

- What value are we selling?
- What are the elements of our offering? What is unique in our offering?
- What value is the customer buying?
- What are the elements of the customer's need?
- Which of the customer's challenges and problems must be solved?

3. Value creation

The third block (3), 'value creation', shows how the industrial company's world is related to its customer's world and how its offering becomes embedded in the customer's context, activities, practices and experiences. Here, the industrial company analyses the possibility of facilitating the customers' value creation, and how they can help their customers reach the goals identified in the first block ('customer's world'). From the customer's point of view, it is important to analyse how value emerges in customer practices, and how the customer achieves the long-term benefits through their own processes. Here, the focus is on analysing how the value is created in the customer's everyday business, and on how the industrial company is able to facilitate its customer's value creation. The questions to be answered include the following:

- How is our offering embedded in the customer's world?
- How can we facilitate customers in reaching their goals?
- How does value emerge in the customer's practices?
- How are the customer's long-term benefits achieved?

4. Interaction and co-production

The fourth block (4), 'interaction and co-production', focuses on the customer's participation in the industrial company's activities and the utilisation of its resources. Here, the key questions relate to how to facilitate the interaction between the industrial company and its customer, and what the customer's mental models of interacting with the industrial company are. In addition, customers' activities and their different use contexts are analysed here. The questions to be answered include the following:

- How can we support customer co-production and the interaction between us and the customer?
- What are the customer's activities during the use of services and resources and different use contexts?
- What are the customer's mental models of interacting with us?

5. Revenue streams and metrics

In the fifth block (5), 'revenue streams and metrics', the industrial company's earnings logic, financial feedback and other benefits are identified. This block also focuses on determining which benefits the customer is willing to pay for. The price is linked to customer value rather than costs. This block also indicates the key performance indicators that verify the value created for the industrial company and its customer. The questions to be answered include the following:

- What is our earnings logic, and how is our financial feedback generated?
- How can we apply customer-value-based pricing?
- What other value do we get, apart from money?
- What are the key performance metrics of our business success?
- Which benefits is the customer actually willing to pay for, and how?
- What is the financial value to the customer?
- What are the key performance indicators of the customer's business, and how are we following them?

6. Key resources

The sixth block (6), 'key resources', focuses on the dynamic, often intangible resources related to the value proposition in question. The core competences are highlighted as key resources. In a service-dominant business, the customer is an important resource, and consequently, the customer's knowledge and skills should also be analysed. The questions to be answered include the following:

- What skills and knowledge do we need to obtain from the customers and other stakeholders?
- What other material and immaterial resources and tools are required?

7. Key partners

The seventh block (7) identifies the 'key partners' and analyses those partners, beyond an industrial company-customer relationship, which are directly required in value creation: here, roles related to value creation, the resources needed and the benefits generated. The questions to be answered include the following:

- Who are our key partners, and what are their roles?
- How do the partners benefit from the cooperation?
- How does the customer experience our partners?
- What kind of partnerships does the customer have, and how should they be taken into account?

8. Mobilising resources and partners

The eighth block (8), 'mobilising resources and partners', focuses on the utilisation and developmental aspects of resources and partners and indicates how knowledge and skills are generated by all stakeholders. This block stresses the integration of resources, which is a central activity of all stakeholders involved in business relationships. The questions to be answered include the following:

- How do we coordinate multi-party value creation?
- How do we utilise and develop partners and resources?
- How can the customer utilise and develop partners and resources?

9. Cost structure

In the ninth block (9), the 'cost structure' of the business model is discussed. In addition to analysing the industrial company's costs and other sacrifices inherent in the business model, the costs and other sacrifices induced for the sake of the customer are analysed. The questions to be answered include the following:

- What are the costs inherent in our business model?
- What are our other sacrifices?
- How would potential cost-cutting impact customer value and experience?
- What costs and other sacrifices are required from the customer?

Conclusion

There is a clear need for managerial approaches that actually help industrial companies develop business models, based on a deep understanding of customers' (and customer's customer's) contexts. The Service Logic Business Model Canvas responds to this need. It forces its users to systematically consider the customer's business with respect to each element of the business model.

Most business model tools address customer needs and value as two of the many elements to be addressed. In comparison, the Service Logic Business Model Canvas places customers' needs, value and contexts at the centre of the business model. In addition, it relates the customer's viewpoint to the industrial company's viewpoint, thus enabling the design of a realistic business model that can be implemented. The testing of the tool in various companies shows that the Service Logic Business Model Canvas is a relevant, easy-to-use and simple tool that can help companies implement a customer-centred business strategy. The tool highlights the importance of deep customer insight, and is designed to be applied to each customer profile separately. By using the framework individually with each relevant customer profile, it is possible to have a deeper understanding of the customer logic of each profile. A separate business model, with all its elements, is designed for each customer profile.

The Service Logic Business Model Canvas functions both as a rapid prototype of a new business model and as a communication tool that quickly shows the company's current (or future) business model. If used in workshops with various manager and employee groups in the industrial company, the canvas can also function as a discussion tool for creating a more customer-centred business culture. It makes people place the customer at the centre of all the elements of a business model.

References

Grönroos, C. and Ravald, A. (2011) Service as business logic: Implications for value creation and marketing. *Journal of Service Management, 22*(1), pp. 5–22.

Heinonen, K., Strandvik, T., Mickelsson, K-J, Edvardsson, B., Sundström, E. and Andersson, P. (2010) A customer dominant logic of service. *Journal of Service Management, 21*(4), pp. 531–548.

Ojasalo, K. 2007. Developing industrial services: An empirical study. *The Business Review*, Cambridge, 7(1), pp. 58–62.

Ojasalo, K., Koskelo, M. and Nousiainen, A.K. (2015) Foresight and service design boosting dynamic capabilities in service innovation. In: Agarwal, R., Selen, W., Roos, G. and Green, R. (Eds.), *The Handbook of Service Innovation* (pp. 193–212). London, UK: Springer.

Ojasalo, K. and Ojasalo, J. (2015) Adapting business model thinking to service logic: An empirical study on developing a service design tool. In: Gummerus, J. and Von Koskull, K. (Eds.), *The Nordic School: Service Marketing and Management for the Future* (pp. 309–333). Helsinki, Finland: CERS, Hanken School of Economics.

Osterwalder, A. and Pigneur, Y. (2010) *Business Model Generation: A Handbook for Visionaries, Game Changers, and Challengers.* Hoboken, NJ: Wiley.

16 The SINCO lab concept

Agile technology-aided experience prototyping toolkit

Simo Rontti

Keywords: Bittium, Santa Park, SINCO, prototyping, case studies

The Service Innovation Corner (SINCO) is a laboratory concept for agile hands-on service development. It was developed at the University of Lapland and has been used and developed in collaboration with dozens of companies, such as Kone, Volkswagen and Danske Bank. In the SINCO lab, service landscapes are simulated quickly with images and sounds, and do not require advanced engineering skills or much preparatory work. Service-scape simulations serve as platforms for experience prototyping in co-creation workshops involving different stakeholders. Mobile devices and applications are used in a creative and agile way with crafted mock-ups and props to demonstrate new ideas. In the SINCO lab, all gadgets, tools and materials are quickly accessible for instant and iterative building. Facilitated co-prototyping sessions at the SINCO lab serve as a communication platform for integrating the service design approach and agile business-development processes.

How can service experiences be prototyped?

In service design, the core of prototyping is users' experience of the service, which consists of touchpoints experienced during the service path. Many touchpoints can be demonstrated as tangible prototypes (e.g. user interface paper mock-ups or cardboard signs). Service prototypes can also involve time (processes or stories), and participants can take on different roles (users, customers, service personnel etc.) to prototype human interactions. The story or case of a service can be demonstrated and simulated as a personal experience through role-playing, which requires activity from the participants. Thus, the facilitator for participants is extremely important because the usage of a service – whether face to face or digital – does not happen in a vacuum, but is strongly tied to users' situational intentions, goals and tasks.

How users experience the service landscape through different senses is also important to the user experience. Audio-visual background simulations and different physical props help to emphasise the situation and context, serving as a scene for the embodied design of interactions and spaces on a 1:1 scale. With the help of existing consumer-priced IT and audio-visual technology, it is possible to easily create various service settings in the laboratory. Technical equipment can replace missing service elements, such as service-scapes, user interfaces, processes and even people. Technology-aided representations stimulate prototyping and help us to understand situational factors, emotional aspects and the viability of new service ideas. The technical equipment available at the SINCO lab makes the immaterial elements of services visible, and allows users to experience these aspects and build new ideas. Using an analogy from industrial design prototyping, SINCO allows users to quickly build 'finnfoam models' of immaterial entities, such as service moments, customer journeys and business concepts.

Why co-prototype in a lab setting?

In many cases, new service ideas can be prototyped easily in real environments following agile and 'quick and dirty' prototyping principles. However, especially in the early phases of the development process, agile prototyping in the lab has many advantages over prototyping in real-life settings. Real service environments (e.g. cafeterias) may be in use or too far away from the development office, or the customer's service path may consist of multiple geographical locations (e.g. airlines and tourism). Confidentiality issues also restrict early prototyping in actual settings. Early high-fidelity prototypes of new solutions along customer journeys are often built as 'Wizard of Oz settings', which is easily done in a lab environment equipped with the tools and devices necessary for this kind of work. From a service staff point of view, settings that are 'too familiar' may blind them to issues that require attention. Service-scape simulation images are taken from everyday working environments, which is a way to make the issues visible to customers. Internet and open multimedia resources enable any atmosphere with background images and sounds to be created in mere seconds.

Service prototyping labs make it possible to toggle among experience, building and analysis modes. In co-design sessions with multiple stakeholders, this advances communication and learning, combining the advantages of both contextual research and focus groups to generate customer insights, and offer participants creativity and safe opportunities to explore ideas. After rough versions of new service concepts have been prototyped iteratively in the SINCO lab, a refined service prototype can be created in a real environment. This is a good opportunity to incorporate video to record the service design's key results.

How can the SINCO approach be used in businesses?

Based on companies' experiences with the SINCO lab and workshop, the following three steps are suggested:

1   Dedicate a space for experience prototyping and creative exploration to support:
   a   Collaboratively sketching an overview of service entities on whiteboards and through doll theatres, Lego play and layout sketching.
   b   Staging a service path for role-playing with simple context simulation, which requires:
      i   Creating a service stage with one or more projector images (with sounds) and a 1:1 scale background image to contextualise the experience.
      ii   Equipping the environment with modifiable props, accessories and multipurpose items and gadgets.
   c   Building 'quick and dirty' mock-ups and fake demos of the ideas, which may involve:
      i   Hands-on prototyping tools and materials, cardboard and paper prototyping.
      ii   Existing consumer-priced audio-visual equipment, IT, mobile devices and applications in order to demonstrate the possibilities of technology.
   d   Documenting, compiling, showing and analysing information in both digital presentations and handwritten notes, which involves:
      i   Plenty of white movable surfaces for notes.
      ii   Projector(s) or TV(s) for easily showing presentations and other digital content.
   e   Hosting, inspiring and enabling efficient facilitation of co-creation workshops for several participants, including internal and external stakeholders.
2   Empower the service-design team as a lab crew and co-prototyping facilitators:
   a   Empower a multi-skilled service design team as a prototyping lab crew with skill-based roles and the potential to develop the lab.
   b   Mandate the team to invite internal and external stakeholders to prototyping sessions, and subcontract service design to bring in expertise from outside the company whenever external and neutral perspectives are pivotal in a project.
3   Embrace a collaborative, experimental and playful prototyping approach and integrate it into the development process as agile sprints:
   a   Identify internal key stakeholders to assemble the best tacit knowledge for co-prototyping.
   b   Designate a key stakeholder team for each project or offering that possesses the best knowledge about the main areas of grassroots service production (e.g. sales, front desk staff, call centre and support), technology and business/development management with an adequate decision-making mandate.
   c   Incentivise attendance to prototyping workshops. Let the co-prototyping workshops become a manifestation of the collaborative working culture and allow creativity, play, safe risk-taking, trial and error, and fun.

d　Choose the place and time for the co-creation workshop depending on its inputs and desired outputs. The double SINCO workshop sprint model syncs well with the double diamond service-design process (Design Council 2007) and agile development processes. The first workshop focuses on reproducing identified challenges and opportunities as experience prototypes, while the second workshop focuses on co-developing and evaluating service concepts. The results of the SINCO workshop sprint may take the form of a detailed service blueprint or be used as a common 'minimum valuable service' that can be experienced (Pinheiro 2014). This may be followed by decision-making concerning service guidelines, development of minimum valuable products (MVPs) of a digital solution that are pivotal to the service or updates to the backlog of an existing service. SINCO workshops serve well as a first strategic sprint in a development project aiming to transform a vague business vision to a tangible prototype of a solution via common customer insights. The typically non-manageable, fuzzy front-end of innovation processes may be clarified through early co-prototyping workshops. At the end of the development process, the service staff responsible for training and education may also work at SINCO, where different customer scenarios can be simulated easily. The SINCO toolkit can be used for service development projects, as well as for enhancing general management and design thinking in an organisation (e.g. by facilitating strategic planning rounds for customer experience prototyping sprints).

SINCO case studies

Bittium (www.bittium.com, previously Elektrobit) is a Finnish company specialising in the development of communications and connectivity solutions. Bittium provides products and customised solutions based on its product platforms, as well as B2B R&D services for customers in various industries. Bittium also offers information security solutions for mobile devices and portable computers. One of their main target groups is official groups such as the police, nurses and fire fighters. In one case, fire fighters' alarm and communication processes were reproduced for the internal R&D team in the SINCO lab, in order to concretise customer insights gathered through interviews and observations, and to realise useful features for the next generation of communication devices. In the second workshop, new business and ecosystem opportunities were explored by prototyping various scenarios related to authorities' safety communication methods, such as mobile emergency-care communication solutions in different contexts. Stakeholders such as product managers, quality assurance employees and R&D engineers participated in developing a solution.

Figure 16.1 Bittium SINCO prototyping workshop.

Santa Park is a Finnish small tourism company that offers a Christmas experience in an underground cave located in Rovaniemi, Finland, which lies in the Arctic Circle. At Santa Park, a visitor can meet elves, ice princesses and Santa Claus in a fantastic environment, and participate in a variety of activities, including Elf School and gingerbread decorating. For our Santa Park service-design project, the first SINCO workshop focused on analysing the current customer journey – a customer travelling from the UK to Lapland and Santa Park – through simulation with the entrepreneur and key service personnel, such as the ticket salespersons and the 'elves'. Other goals of the workshop were to explore, experiment and understand the technological possibilities of extending the in-place experience through digital channels to the phases before and after the actual park visit, and engage in collaboration to begin the ideation phase. In the second SINCO workshop, the service concepts were tested and refined with internal stakeholders before conducting a separate concept prototype test, with customers using interface mock-ups and other touchpoint prototypes built in the actual service environment (the Santa Park cave).

Conclusion

Even though the SINCO toolkit may seem to be a way to design spaces or an investment in devices, it is, more importantly, a working approach and design-management tool. The physical spaces and equipment and organisational culture should support collaborative experimentation and the concretisation of ideas and opportunities from a customer experience perspective early and often during the development process. This is in opposition to speculating 'the facts'

Figure 16.2 Santa Park workshop at SINCO.

in a negotiation room, and including concrete elements only when a 'truth', based on organisation-driven assumptions, has been presented in PowerPoint or Excel, and investments have been made. SINCO, as a space and set of equipment with an inspirational facilitation team, offers a practical toolkit for putting service design thinking into action and enhancing creativity and stakeholder communication in development projects.

References

Design Council (2007) *11 Lessons: Managing Design in Global Brands.* Retrieved from www.designcouncil.org.uk/sites/default/files/asset/document/ElevenLessons_Design_ Council%20%282%29.pdf (accessed 23 December 2015).

Pinheiro, T. (2014) *The Service Startup: Design Thinking Gets Lean.* Hayakawa: Altabooks & Createspace.

17 The Design Impact Chart

A tool for scoping your service design project

Erik Widmark and Susanna Nissar

Keywords: Design Impact Chart, stakeholders, process, action

Service design projects are human-centred, iterative and co-creative, and require that users and stakeholders work collaboratively to turn challenges into tangible solutions. However, depending on what you apply the service design methodology to, the outcome can be anything from improved services to new business strategies, organisational changes (in larger companies) or the redesign of an entire system. Service design is thus used not only for creating services but also as a tool to frame and solve any complex problem with multiple stakeholders and perspectives.

With new applications of the methodology, the complexity of service design projects has increased exponentially. This makes it even more important to ensure that everybody involved in a service design project shares a common view of the purpose and scope. To help organisations frame their service design initiatives, we developed the Design Impact Chart. The purpose of this tool is to serve as a common ground for stakeholders when defining the type of project to which they will apply the service design methodology, thus helping maintain the scope of the project. By using this framework, we hope that each service design initiative can reach its full potential to create great experiences for design touchpoints, services, organisations or systems.

Variables of the Design Impact Chart

The Design Impact Chart consists of a matrix with two axes: the zoom level axis and the stakeholder complexity axis. We have used public transport to exemplify what we mean when we describe the tool.

Zoom level axis

The variables of the zoom axis range from the micro (one action) to the macro (one experience) level. In general, one can say that the more you zoom in, the more detailed and specific your solution will be, and the more you zoom out, the more strategic your take on the overall experience will be, and the more likely it is that solutions will come in the form of guidelines rather than detailed solutions.

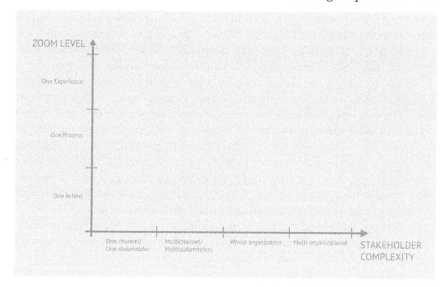

Figure 17.1 Variables of the Design Impact Chart.

In general, it is good to use service design from a zoomed-out perspective to set strategies and guidelines, and then zoom in and work on the details. If you define the strategies, you are more likely to get the touchpoints right.

The most zoomed-in level of a service design project involves designing actions in a service. Actions, as we define them, typically have no inherent value to customers, but could be a vital component in the overall service. Services typically consist of several actions that work together in order to create value for the user. Using the example of public transport, an action could be paying for a metro ticket. In this micro perspective, a service design project would focus on optimising a defined component according to the user's needs and logic.

The one-process level involves what most people would consider to be a service. A service is a series of actions that are organised into a relevant sequence, such as: choose a metro ticket; pay for the ticket; receive the ticket; and use the ticket. A service design project at this level would collect insights about users and the context in order to define and co-design the actions within the service, and then weave them together in a relevant and logical way.

The experience level is focused on making sure all the processes (services) coexist and cooperate in unison. In a public transport context, this could involve: selecting the type of public transport you will take; planning your route; choosing, paying for, receiving and using your ticket; and finding your final destination.

Channel/stakeholder axis

The variables on the channel/stakeholder axis range from a single channel to multiple organisations. In general, the fewer stakeholders that are involved, the more straightforward the project will be, since there are fewer perspectives that must be considered, causing the decision process to be shorter and less complicated. On the other hand, the more channels and stakeholders that are involved, the higher the potential impact on the users' overall experience.

When we design for one channel, we work with one aspect of how the customer interacts with the organisation. A channel could be a smartphone app. These projects typically have low stakeholder complexity, and there's often a defined manager in charge of making most of the decisions for the channel. The desired outcome and effect is improved usability and user experience within that channel. These types of projects usually produce important components of users' experience with a service provider. However, since customers usually interact with several channels, these projects will rarely have a great impact on the overall customer experience.

Designing for several channels means that we are involving multiple stakeholders within the organisation in order to deliver a coherent and relevant service across channels – such as across all digital channels. The challenge in this type of project is to help customers understand the role of various channels and stakeholders. A powerful tool for creating this common platform of understanding is the customer journey map. By centring your efforts on customers' needs, processes and contexts, you will generate a neutral platform for ideation and evaluation of service improvements and innovation.

Organisational design means designing all channels internally and externally based on the needs of the customer; in other words, ensuring customer-centricity in the entire organisation. In our example, the organisation could be the company running the metro trains. When designing all channels, stakeholder complexity increases exponentially, and there is a great need to involve both upper management and staff who interact with customers, in order to generate a common understanding of the organisation's goals and the customers' needs. Since there are so many stakeholders and perspectives, a great tool for maintaining common ground is the service map. The service map is a tool that shows both customers' perception of a service or system, as well as the organisational structure. With this map, the organisation can make strategic decisions based on customers' values and needs, while prioritising and tracing the implications of these decisions for the organisation and the various channels that are involved. The effects of large-scale organisational transformations normally do not become apparent for 2–3 years, so it is good to prepare for some 'low-hanging fruit' success stories along the way to keep staff members' spirits up and show progress. Those 'low-hanging fruits' could be small changes within a channel that will be highly appreciated by customers.

When addressing challenges on a multi-organisational level, stakeholder complexity is extremely high, but the potential benefit for customers is enormous. In these types of projects, there is a need to involve several different actors that influence customers' experience of the wider system. In our public transport scenario, a multi-organisational project could involve the metro company, the bus company and the commuter train company. With so many different interests and agendas, a great tool for unifying the various stakeholders

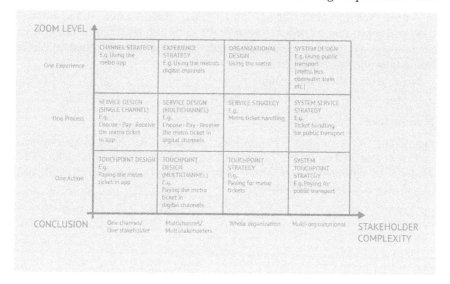

Figure 17.2 The Design Impact Chart.

is an eco-system map. The eco-system map illustrates the role of the system in users' lives and shows the layers of actors and factors that influence the experience and function of the system.

Conclusion

Generally speaking, the further up and to the right your projects are on the Design Impact Chart, the more impact the results will have on overall customer experience. The closer to the origin of the axes the projects are, the easier they will be to manage and the more tangible the results will be, but the more limited their impact will be on overall customer experience. In order to manage and create a coherent customer experience, you will need to initiate projects within all areas of the Design Impact Chart.

If you or your organisation already have experience with service design methods, and want to have a greater effect on customer experience, we recommend that you start with service design initiatives in the upper right-hand corner of the Design Impact Chart (experience strategy, organisational design or system design, if applicable). These types of service design projects will typically generate strategic guidelines and priorities for you to manage your customer experience. Once this is in place, you can implement these guidelines and priorities for all projects affecting customer experience.

If your organisation is new to the service design methodology, it is recommended that you start with a project with few stakeholders and little complexity. These types of projects are typically easier to grasp and are a great way to learn the processes while building internal successes, which are often needed to obtain support from the rest of the organisation.

Within each area of the Design Impact Chart, there is a need to use different tools and approaches in order to achieve the optimum results for every project. Some suggested tools are mentioned briefly here, and more information can be found in service design literature.

Now, go out there and design!

References

Osterwalder, A., Pigneur, Y., Bernarda, G. and Smith, A. (2015) *Value Proposition Design: How to Create Products and Services Customers Want*. Hoboken, NJ: John Wiley.

Thaler, R.H. and Sunstein, C.R. (2009) *Nudge: Improving Decisions about Health, Wealth, and Happiness*. London: Penguin.

18 Video in service design

Heikki Tikkanen, Titta Jylkäs,
Jaana Jeminen and Satu Miettinen

Keywords: video, prototyping, communicating, documenting

Service design videos are a great way to develop and share service concepts and value offerings within the corporation and among stakeholders. Most importantly, they can be used to strengthen the human element and emotional aspects of designing and using a service or a product.

Video is a complex media. It delivers content through text, images, sound and timing. Thus, it is well suited for capturing and communicating concepts ranging from tangible and small-scale ideas to large and abstract concepts, and from very personal concepts to those that may affect millions of people. Video can tell not only *what* but also *how* and *why* something is said or done; it can deliver very precise messages; and is effortless to follow, so it can be 'poured on' to people rather than requiring them to 'pick up' the information. Video makes ideas and experiences tangible and leaves little room for misunderstandings.

Video is an agile method for storing and communicating information related to a design case. One can either share the raw material of an authentic event straight away or take time to plan and edit the video thoroughly to suit its intended audience and desired impact. Both methods are useful in certain situations. However, videos should not be made for the sake of doing so. To create a truly useful service design video, first consider what impact you want it to have on your design case or stakeholders, and make this the single goal of the video.

The following are examples of video goals and the work required for each of them:

- Convey what customers feel about the service: document and share research data; do this in the fastest way; 'shoot and share'.
- Reveal what was produced in the last workshop and how: concretise methods and results; do it quickly; 'shoot, cut and share'.
- Express why management should support this new service concept: appeal to decision-makers; requires planning; 'plan, shoot, cut and share'.

Video is a fast and comprehensive method for storing material about customer insights or the results of design tasks. In this sense, it might not be a bad idea to record nearly everything while working on the case. Going through a large amount of material to find something specific later on takes time, but all the research will be saved in an authentic format. Proper archiving is very important.

It is easy to learn how to create videos. With today's intuitive technology and the variety of online guidance videos, tools are available to anyone with Internet access. Videos are also a very affordable method of communication. They are also affordable for sharing and publishing the finished material.

What is the role of video in service design?

Video can be used in service design for:

- Documenting: customer insights and discoveries obtained through interviews, observation, probes and co-creation.
- Prototyping: acting out a user story, role-playing to solve current problems, using ideation to find solutions and filming inspirational material.
- Communicating: method for establishing consensus between stakeholders or disseminating the design results.

Video has its own possibilities in each phase of the design process (discover, define, develop and deliver). It can be used either as a one-time working method – for example, to quickly produce a video prototype of a certain service – or it can be used constantly throughout all phases. Continuous filming during observation sessions can serve as an inspirational tool for designers during the discovery and definition phases to determine what was observed and what can be learned about it (Ylirisku and Buur 2007).

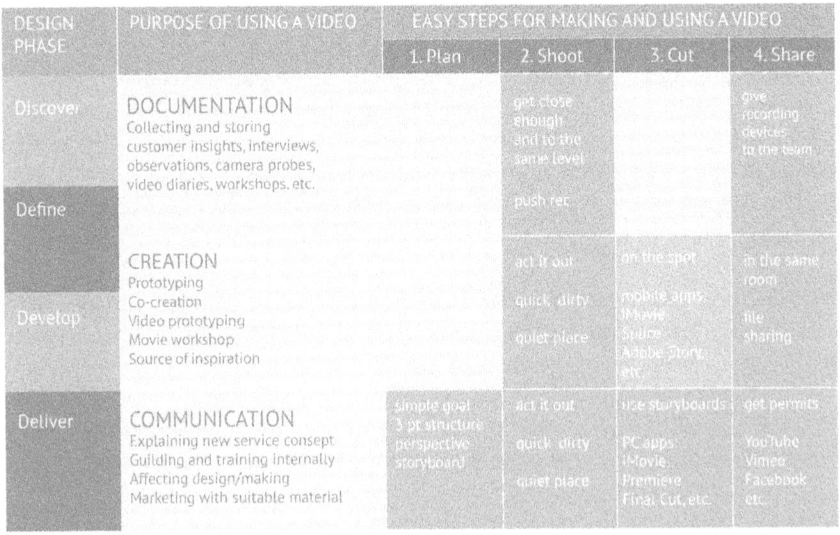

DESIGN PHASE	PURPOSE OF USING A VIDEO	EASY STEPS FOR MAKING AND USING A VIDEO			
		1. Plan	2. Shoot	3. Cut	4. Share
Discover	DOCUMENTATION Collecting and storing customer insights, interviews, observations, camera probes, video diaries, workshops. etc.		get close enough and to the same level		give recording devices to the team
Define			push rec		
Develop	CREATION Prototyping Co-creation Video prototyping Movie workshop Source of inspiration		act it out quick dirty quiet place	on the spot mobile apps: iMovie Splice Adobe Story etc.	in the same room file sharing
Deliver	COMMUNICATION Explaining new service consept Guilding and training internally Affecting design/making Marketing with suitable material	simple goal 3 pt structure perspective storyboard	act it out quick dirty quiet place	use storyboards PC apps: iMovie Premiere Final Cut, etc.	get permits YouTube Vimeo Facebook etc.

Figure 18.1 Using video in service design.

In the discovery phase, video helps to obtain deep, holistic customer insights. Optimally, it can capture and communicate the customer experience in a nuanced way. Compared to written observations or interview outcomes, seeing and hearing authentic reactions creates deeper understanding and empathy towards the customer. In this sense, video is a strong witness and can erase doubt by fulfilling the need to 'see it to believe it'.

Video is a way to share detailed understandings effectively. It enables people to return to past service moments as if they were happening again. Although video is usually not used until it is time to tell stakeholders what has been designed and why, it works as an effective communication method in every phase of the design process, both internally and externally.

In the definition and development phases of the service or product design process, video can be used as more than just a way to record authentic customer insights in the discovery phase, or to communicate design outcomes when the process is almost over. Video can and should be used more and much earlier in the process, rather than just for replacing or supplementing the final presentation slides or written reports with moving images.

How should it be done?

The simplest way to think about using video in service design is as an addition to (and, sometimes, a replacement for) text, photos or other media. If you can write, draw, take a photo or sketch a model, you can make a video. You have what it takes. Most effectively, video can be used as a natural part of design, like writing and drawing. It will take time to make using a camera or phone a routine, but once you grasp the concept, it will be hard not to do it.

Service design videos can be useful even as clips that are recorded when talking with a customer and then shared with the team. This requires only two steps: shooting and sharing. In this way, it is similar to taking and sharing notes or a photo, but it takes less effort and provides more information. For more complex videos that require more work, use the following guidelines.

1. Keep it simple

Advertising studios know that a good video has only one goal: to make people buy what they see. What is the one purpose of your video? What do you want the viewer to feel, think and do after seeing it? Always record for a reason. Write down your goal in one clear sentence.

2. Plan the structure

Once you have a clear goal, determine what kind of story will support it best and what kind of footage you can build that story with. A story has a beginning, middle and end. Each part engages the viewer with your service in a different way. The beginning should arouse interest, perhaps by presenting a problem.

The middle should communicate the main statement of the video, such as a solution to a problem. The ending should call the viewer to take the action. This three-part story structure aligns well with the before, during and after phases of a service experience. Write your three parts on paper to make them tangible to concretise your story.

3. Define the perspective

Select a point of view when planning the story. Who is your most important audience? How can you appeal to them? Towards whom do you want them to feel empathy? Whose point of view do you want to share? Write these things down; remembering them helps you to decide what to film and how to film. Even the camera angle and picture size affect how we feel about someone we see in a video. When you look down on someone with the camera, is it intentional or accidental? Basic photography skills will help you craft better videos, and you can quickly learn more about such techniques online.

4. Create a storyboard

Although it is not needed for all videos, a storyboard can be extremely helpful when creating complex videos. It is comprised of a set of rough images that show each 'shot' of the video in chronological order, describing the shots' size, angle and action. It is useful and affordable to create different versions on paper before recording. Again, a basic knowledge of film composition will help you improve the emotional impact and continuity of the storyboard. You can either plan the composition beforehand in the storyboard, or record many versions of each shot and pick the best ones when editing (Quesenbery and Brooks 2010). Filming without a pre-planned storyboard is also possible. For this, develop the habit of filming a 'B-roll', or footage of something other than the subject of your interview or observation that is relevant to the story. The B-roll helps you to fill uninteresting or low-quality clips of the 'A-roll', or the main footage.

5. Set and shoot quick and dirty

In service design, video is a tool for communicating service concepts and their human elements. It appeals through its content, not through high-end production quality. If you lack something, replace it with whatever you have. A chair does not have to be a chair; it can be a car or an office. Use your creativity to build the environment and action that effectively concretises your concept and delivers your main message (Buchenau and Suri 2000).

Conclusion

The production quality of videos for service design is not nearly as important as their content: people and their stories. There is no need for Hollywood aesthetics, but there must be a clear message to ensure the desired impact on your target audience. Some online video-marketing studies have proven that 'user-created content' makes viewers more likely to take the desired actions than professional advertisements.

Try allowing customers to make videos. Use it as a 'first-person probe' rather than a conventional video diary. Let customers or other stakeholders show you their reality and point the camera towards the things that are important to them. Maybe even put a Go-Pro on their forehead.

Use positive customer videos to market your business online. These can be obtained, for example, while doing customer interviews for a service design case. Before publishing, remember to get permission from the people you film and make sure they know the purpose for which you are using the video. Quick and well-considered questions reveal honest and spontaneous opinions, as interviewees have little time to think about their answers. Hesitation and ignorance, as well as satisfaction and appreciation, are obvious on video.

References

Buchenau, M. and Suri, J.F. (2000, August) Experience Prototyping. In: *Proceedings of the 3rd Conference on Designing Interactive Systems: Processes, Practices, Methods, and Techniques* (pp. 424–433). New York: ACM.

Quesenbery, W. and Brooks, K. (2010) *Storytelling for User Experience: Crafting Stories for Better Design*. New York: Rosenfeld Media.

Yliriksu, S.P. and Buur, J. (2007) *Designing with Video: Focusing the User-Centred Design Process*. London: Springer Science & Business Media.

Index